John Allen:

Michigan's
Pioneer Promoter

by Kit Lane

Pavilion
Press
P.O. Box 250
Douglas, Mi 49406

John Allen
1796 - 1851

The Vision

John Allen was described in a 1906 Washtenaw County history as, "a man of exceedingly hopeful disposition." In similar language, Orlando Stephenson, in his 1927 history of Ann Arbor called him a "man of dreams."

Some of his dreams were more successful than others. He was early recognized as a co-founder and driving force behind the settlement at Ann Arbor. But he had a hand in many other Michigan settlements as well, notably Mason in Van Buren County (which later became Lawrence), Spring Arbor, South Haven, Meridian, Grand Haven, and Richmond in Allegan County, which was planned to be the grandest of them all. In addition he held land, "thousands of acres" his official biography reports, in Eaton, Ingham, Calhoun, Washtenaw, Van Buren, Allegan, Jackson, and Kalamazoo counties, and perhaps others.

Settlement in the Michigan Territory spread slowly. Missionaries and fur traders came in the late 1600's, and the first contingent of soldiers and workers arrived at Detroit in 1701, but it was another century before much effort was made to move inland and open up new areas. The vast forests that covered the land made farmers think twice about the work needed to clear land, and others were delayed waiting for surveyors to complete their mapping and for Indian treaties to give the United States land office a title they felt sufficient to open new territory for sale.

By the 1820s a new breed of organizer-speculator had appeared on the Michigan scene. These men were generally second or third generation North Americans who had lived first in the east, most often New York State, and who came west with some skills in pioneering, usually either farming or milling, and had a nest egg to purchase land on which they would plat a village. Their hope was for a quick profit selling small village lots to those who wished to settle in communities in the interior of Michigan.

Unlike many other land speculators of the era, Allen saw the importance of improvements to attract settlers and made efforts to provide mills, roads and mail routes. If his financial resources did not always measure up to his vision -- that was a common problem of the times. Some communities, especially those with a special reason for being, like a county seat, or an important transfer point on the river, grew rapidly, and the owners would often receive their investment back one hundred fold. Some villages grew rapidly for a time but lost population when living patterns changed. The railroads made ghost towns out of many riverbank villages, and other settlements founded around a central sawmill or other industry, disappeared following disastrous fires -- a common occurrence in the days of log cabins with open fireplaces. In addition many "paper towns" sprang up around Michigan. They were settlements founded in hope, and well documented in detailed and flamboyant maps, which never progressed beyond the paper dream. John Allen knew all three circumstances.

The population of Michigan in 1820 was barely over 9,000. A handful of these individuals are mentioned over and over in the early histories. They were the shapers and movers of their times. They led the armies, fought the federal government for legislation that would benefit their territory, located the county seats, were actively engaged in fur trading, milling, shop keeping, started the churches, organized the schools, and ran for public office. John Allen was one of these.

Some of his contemporaries included: Stevens T. Mason, Michigan's "boy governor"; Lewis Cass, general, territorial governor, U. S. Cabinet Secretary, and Senator; Father Gabriel Richard, Roman Catholic priest and missionary, founder of the first newspaper in Michigan, delegate to Congress; Louis Campau, founder of Grand Rapids, and fur trader; Lucius Lyon, surveyor, politician, mining engineer, founder of several settlements; William Woodbridge, lawyer, judge and governor; Rix Robinson, fur trader, senator, founder of Ada and Grand Haven; Flavius T. Littlejohn, lawyer, politician,

5

writer; and B. H. Packard, physician, and founder of Albion College. What they had in common was a vision for the new State of Michigan, and the drive to tend that vision.

Even among this distinguished company John Allen stood out as the eternal optimist. To the end he remained convinced that gold and prosperity, riches and fame, would yet be his -- just over the next mountain.

Virginia Roots

John Allen was born in Augusta County, Virginia, May 17, 1796, probably at the family homestead on the road to Winchester, north of the village of Staunton, just to the west of the Blue Ridge Mountains in the valley of the Shenandoah River. The area is now located in the northwest corner of the state of Virginia about 50 miles east of the western boundary. Prior to the creation of West Virginia in 1863, it was nearer the heart of Virginia.

In 1796 Augusta County was just beginning to settle into the business of being a part of the United States of American after nearly a century of colonial rule, changing governors at the whim of the British monarch. George Washington was just finishing his second term as president.

Traditionally the first expedition to visit the area of Augusta County was led by Governor Alexander Spotswood in 1716, to investigate the lands of Virginia west of the Blue Ridge Mountains. (It is argued that woodsmen had earlier penetrated the country, but their visit was of little political importance.) A group of Germans were the earliest true settlers, arriving before 1729, and John Lewis and family came the summer of 1732 and established the town of Staunton.

By the time the first settlers arrived there were no longer any Indian tribes resident in the valley, but the area was used as a "hunting ground and as a highway for belligerent parties of different nations, in their military expeditions against each other," according to an Augusta County history. "In consequence of the almost continuous hostilities between the northern and southern Indians, these expeditions were very frequent and tended to somewhat retard settlement of the Valley, and render a residence in it, for some time, insecure and unpleasant." The earliest history of the west Virginia area is filled with tales of massacres and scalpings. Treaties with the chiefs of the Six Nations completed in 1744 and 1752 were rendered ineffective in June of 1754, when settlers, conditioned by Indian atrocities, massacred 13 visiting braves. Much unrest existed between the settlers and several Indian tribes for the next decade, with the last documented Indian attack on the area taking place in 1764. The men of Augusta County continued to battle the Indians on the frontier farther west, including the famous battle of Point Pleasant on the Ohio River. In 1794, the Indian question in the east was settled decisively by Gen. Anthony Wayne at the Battle of Fallen Timbers on the Maumee River in what would later be Ohio.

The Allens had arrived in Virginia

from Ireland before 1750. The patriarch of the American Allens was William, who had three sons. James (the grandfather of John Allen of Michigan) was born in Ireland and crossed the ocean at seven years of age. Hugh and John were born after the family's arrival in America. John Allen was said to have been lost while serving as a lieutenant under General Edward Braddock during the French and Indian War. Both James and Hugh served with a local regiment under Col. Charles Lewis and saw action in 1774 at Point Pleasant where troops of Colonial Virginia, under the command of Gen. Andrew Lewis, brother of Col. Charles, fought hostile Indians along the Ohio River. Hugh was lost in that skirmish and buried beside Col. Lewis, also a battle casualty. James placed a stone on the grave.

James Allen lived at a place later called Willow Spout, where the Middle River crossed the main north-south road in the Shenandoah valley. This road was sometimes called the Great Philadelphia Wagon Road. By 1750, although still ungraded, it reached from Augusta, Georgia, to Philadelphia, Pennsylvania. (In the 1830's the road was paved with macadam and called the Valley Turnpike.) James established a mill on the Middle River just to the south of the house, and farmed vast areas in the bottomland and to the west of his house.

James and Hugh Allen married sisters, daughters of John Anderson, a native of Ireland. Hugh had three sons, John, William and Hugh, who left Virginia at an early date for Kentucky. The

9

Kentucky county of Allen was named for Hugh's son, John.

James Allen and his wife Margaret (Anderson) Allen had ten children: Jane, who married Capt. James Trimble and went to Kentucky in 1783 accompanied by the sons of Hugh Allen and many others; Ann, wife of Col. George Poage; Elizabeth, wife of the Rev. John McCue; Rebecca, wife of Major John Crawford; Margaret, wife of Major William Bell; Mary, wife of Col. Nicholas Lewis who removed to Kentucky; Nancy, wife of Capt. Samuel Frame; Sarah, wife of James Bell; William, who married Susan Bell of Kentucky having removed there with the others in 1783; and James Allen Jr. who was married to Elizabeth Tate, and was the father of seven children, including John Allen, later of Michigan.

The Tate family had come from Ireland to Pennsylvania, and then to Virginia arriving in 1745. The first emigrant had four sons. Robert, the youngest, married Margaret McClung, and had ten children, including Elizabeth. An 1883 Augusta County history recorded that the family was, "noted for its piety, industry and public spirit."

It is likely that John attended the Staunton Academy as a youth. It was founded in 1792 about 10 miles south of his home. Education was important to the Allens; his grandfather had been on the committee in 1775 to solicit sub-scriptions for the Augusta Academy, but the school was later moved to Lexing-ton, Virginia, "because there was no one in Staunton to take the management, and it was uncertain whether there ever would be." The Augusta Academy later developed into Washington and Lee University. The Staunton Academy operated as a private school for 70 years. After the school closed in 1873 the building was used for a time by the public school system.

During his early married life the younger James lived in log houses not far from the family plantation on the north-south road. After the death of his father in 1810, as the only son who remained in Virginia, James moved his growing family to the larger brick home near the mill on the north bank of the Middle River just north of what would later be called the village of Verona. The large rectangular house was still standing in 1988, well-preserved and little changed. A white wooden structure to the rear of the house, used in the early days as a residence for slaves, also remained. Behind the house and outbuildings the land falls off abruptly and a rocky escarpment forms a natural corral, probably a popular play area for James and Elizabeth's seven children.

The house was to figure prominently in area history during the Civil War. The Shenandoah valley was invaded frequently during the war and on one foray Gen. Philip Sheridan used it as his headquarters, with Gen. George Armstrong Custer staying in another house just across the river. On arrival Sheridan ordered his men to set fire to the mill. As the fire was beginning to burn the owner of the property at the time, Samuel Cline, rushed out with papers

The Allen homestead near Staunton

proving that he was in sympathy with the north. The general reversed his orders and charged his men with putting the fire out. The general himself was said to have helped.

On November 2, 1815, at the age of nineteen, John Allen was married to seventeen-year-old Polly Crawford, the daughter of James and Mary (Crawford) Crawford. James Allen "being disposed to aid son John, who was then about establishing himself in life" made him an advancement of slaves and property estimated at $2,000. Polly had recently inherited some Virginia property from her father's estate as well as 1600 acres in Green County, Kentucky. The youngest of the Crawford children she was born after her father's death in 1798.

John and Polly's first child, James
Crawford Allen, was born in 1816,
followed by a daughter, Elizabeth, in
1819. On May 6, 1819 Polly died leaving
John with two small children. The 1820
census shows that his household included
one female under 10, one male under 10,
two males between 16 and 26 (himself and
possibly a brother or hired man), and
six slaves.

The same 1820 census lists the
family of Col. James Allen as one male
between 16 and 18, one male between 16
and 26, and one male over 45, also a
female under 10, two between 10 and 16,
one between 16 and 26, and one between
26 and 45, plus nine slaves. John's
father was a colonel in the local
militia and his title was usually used
in Augusta County, even in official
records to avoid confusion with Dr.
James Allen, a distant cousin, who prac-
ticed medicine for many years in the
Stone Church area just north of the
Allen family farm.

Children born to Col. James Allen
and his wife in addition to John were
William, who married into the Poage
family; Mary, wife of Capt. John Welsh;
Margaret, second wife of Maj. William
Poage of Augusta, one of their daughters
was later the wife of James A. Walker,
Lieutenant-Governor of Virginia; Nancy,
wife of Charles Lewis, related to the
first settler in Augusta County; Sarah,
wife of George Mayse of Bath County, and
James Turner Allen, who later migrated
with the family to Michigan.

In *Sketches of Virginia, Historical*

and Biographical published in 1850, author William Henry Foote relates an experience of John's father that occurred some time in the late 1700's. According to Foote, James attended a series of meetings held by noted evangelist Rev. William Graham and, as he later explained, "he had lived without religion until after he was head of a family, having a wife and some children. When it pleased God to open his blind eyes and show him his lost condition, his convictions were awful; and increased to such a great degree that his spirits were dried up and his bodily frame greatly weakened. . . When he was enabled to believe understandingly, his joy was as great as his terror was before."

During another visit James once asked Rev. Graham how long it took him to compose a sermon. After some moments silence the preacher said gravely, "About twenty years." A student explained, "When it was his object to elucidate some difficult point, it was his custom to open his trenches, so to speak, at a great distance, removing out of the way every obstacle, until at last they could not easily avoid acquiescence in the conclusion to which he wished to bring them."

In 1819 James, burdened with more than $16,000 worth of debt, conveyed to sons John and William most of his worldly possessions including: "500 acres of land, eight slaves, fifteen hundred bushels of wheat, two wagons and harnesses complete, fifty head of cattle, one hundred sheep, one hundred head of

hogs, and a number of farming utensils."
In exchange John and William were to
manage the land and stock so as to pay
off their father's debt.

On June 7, 1821, John was married to
Ann Isabella (Barry) McCue, widow of Dr.
William McCue of Lexington, Virginia.
Ann had been born in Staunton, January
22, 1797, the daughter of Thomas and Ann
Isabella (Smith) Barry. When she was
nine days old her mother died, and her
father, a successful merchant, died before her third birthday. Her uncle,
Andrew Barry, was named her guardian,
and she was cared for by Patsy (Dold)
McDowell in Staunton for three years before being sent to Ireland to the home
of her grandmother, Sarah (McKim) Barry.
She returned to America with her grandmother and an aunt in 1807 and was later
sent to a boarding school in Baltimore
where she studied French, etiquette and
letter writing

At the age of 16 she was married to
Dr. William McCue, son of the Rev. John
McCue who was for many years pastor of
the Tinkling Springs Church near
Staunton. Her Uncle Andrew had taken for
a second wife Mary (called Polly), the
eldest of the McCue daughters. John
Allen's Aunt Elizabeth, one of his
father's elder sisters, was the wife of
Rev. McCue. After finishing his medical
education William returned to Augusta
County and lived with his sister and
Andrew Barry at their new brick home on
Mossy Creek where he met Ann. After
their marriage they moved to Lexington,
Virginia, where their two sons, John and
Thomas W., were born, and Dr. McCue died

15

November 18, 1818.

The will left by Dr. McCue named his brother, James A. McCue, guardian of his two sons. They were taken to the McCue home in Mt. Solon, and there joined their cousins. "We were some size before we knew we were not brothers," James's son, J. Marshall McCue, wrote later. In 1822 Ann filed a bill in Augusta courts before she was able to obtain her dower rights. (The McCue men seemed to have a tradition of being less-than-generous to their widows. The will of John McCue that was filed in 1817 gave his widow,"uncontrolled use of the house in which she now lives. She may not move slaves from the farm, or hire them out. If she chooses to move in with one of the other children, she has no claim to any more of my estate, real or personal, but her clothes, a well-furnished bed, a good horse and saddle.")

John brought his new bride to the large brick house overlooking the mill. Their only child, a daughter Sarah Ann, was born May 10, 1823.

By 1822 John and William had made little progress in paying off their father's debt. William relinquished all right to any of the property or responsibility for the debt, and John undertook to go it alone. Not only had the debt not been paid, it had in fact been increased. A fragment of a letter from John later entered into evidence in chancery court urges his father to pay the three largest debts, totaling over $10,000 and adds, "I could pay the rest. Compare my circumstances at present with

16

what they were when I undertook   with
William. I then owned the same property
and owed $4,000. This comes to the point
to prove my own folly. Not that I regret
what I have done, for I feel conscious
of   having   done   to   the   best   of   my
abilities, encouraged by the   reflection
that   I   had   taken   them   from   your
shoulders, a burden I always considered
as   too heavy for you. How does the case
stand now? Those shoulders having   been
rested.   I   wish you to think and calcu-
late the affairs and be ready to   under-
take   that   which   you think proper as I
have no voice but necessity."

On July 28, 1823,   the   debts   were
transferred   back   to   James. He was now
bound by debts of $28,000,   including   a
number   of John's notes for which he had
stood security.

Some time after this   transfer   took
place John   left Augusta County with a
herd of   cattle.   Whether these   were
cattle from his father's herd to be sold
to satisfy some of   the   debt,   or   some
other purchased on credit, is not clear.
A portion of the herd was to   be   driven
to Richmond   to   complete   payment on a
carriage he   had   purchased;   the   rest,
according to family tradition, were sold
at the stockyards in Baltimore.

Then John Allen simply vanished.

Heading North

How much planning and forethought went into John's sudden foray north with the proceeds of the cattle sale has been a matter of much speculation, early by family members and creditors, later by historians. J. Marshall McCue wrote in his memoirs that "The impression became a general one that he had been assassinated, in which his parents shared, or seemed to, at least." While the elder Allens despaired of ever seeing their son again, John's wife, Ann, took the infant Sarah and went to live at the home of James McCue, the brother of her first husband, who had custody of her two children by that marriage.

John made his way north, how quickly or directly is not known, nor is it known when he arrived in Buffalo, New York. There is, in the John Allen manuscript collection in the Burton Historical Collection in Detroit, a letter addressed to "Mr. J. Allen of Virginia, Carrols', Buffaloe," dated October 10, 1823, but a note on it in Allen's handwriting indicated that it was received in Buffalo in November, 1823, raising some speculation about whether anyone knew he was coming. The letter was written by M. T. Williams who gives his address as "Rathbun's, Buffaloe," and its contents give the impression that the two had recently had a conversation, or at least exchanged correspondence. It reads in part: "Joseph Howard at Delaware will forward to you a map of Delaware District with entries marked up to the time of sending. The price for the map is $1.50. If you go to Woods County, call on Dr. Conant and Mr. Hunt at village of Maumee. They are gentlemen on whose information you may rely...I should be grateful to hear from you -- shall be at Columbus during the months of December and January -- after which Cincinnati" and he adds a P. S.: "Gov. Cass and Col. Hunt at Detroit will be glad to afford you all information they can -- I would advise you to call on them without ceremony." All of the places he mentions in the main body of the letter are in Ohio. Micajah T. Williams later became one of the founders of Toledo.

Another letter from a Mr. Harris of the Seneca Mission near Buffalo gives some insight as to where the man from Virginia, away from his home and family may have spent Christmas. It is dated December 29, 1823, addressed simply to "Mr. Allen, Buffalo," and thanks him for the "great obligation you have conferred upon Mrs. Harris and myself for the seasonable and truly valuable donation with which you have presented the mission." The notation by John on the outer wrap reads, "on donation sent them of goods, etc."

It was during his stay in Buffalo

that he first became acquainted with the Moseley family, later of Ann Arbor. A letter from William A. Moseley, outlines how John played cupid for a Buffalo couple during his time there.

The Asa Mills family, originally of Connecticut, met John Allen in Buffalo, and later came to Ann Arbor to settle. According to an account published in a Kalamazoo County history, Loren and Willard Mills, two of the fourteen children, were serving as apprentice tailors in the shop of Deacon Abner Bryant in Buffalo: "One day a man of commanding personal appearance and pleasing manners came into the shop to get his clothes mended. From him they heard an interesting and vivid description of the beautiful region where Ann Arbor now is. The stranger was John Allen of Virginia, the founder of Ann Arbor. Pleased with the report of this country it was decided that Simeon and Augustus should go in advance and spy out the land for the family." They arrived first, when the settlement at Ann Arbor was just three months old. If this recollection is correct, then John knew before he left Buffalo where in Michigan he was headed. Since it was written many years after the incident, most historians have discounted the details.

Micajah Williams was encouraging when it came to John's plans for settlement, but less so about wintertime travel on the lakes. "I am fearful you will have an unpleasant journey by water to Detroit," he wrote. "Hope, however, for the best, and shall be rejoiced to hear from you and of your welfare."

In January, when John was ready to leave, winter ice made the Great Lakes impassable, and he made the trip on foot, apparently through Canada. After he had reported his safe arrival, W. Williams, a friend from Buffalo who may have been host during his stay, wrote: "Your favor of (January) the 27th was received two days since, and believe me nothing could have given me more pleasure than the hearing of your safe arrival in Detroit. I did not at all like the scape galley look of that fellow who took you from here. I know we do not always judge correctly of men, but if that fellow is an honest man I can only say, God does not always write a legible hand."

In Detroit John Allen met Elisha Walker Rumsey (he was occasionally accused of adding the Elisha to his name to escape a shady past; whatever the truth in this, he was usually called Walker). The two men apparently had similar ideas concerning the fortune to be made in land speculation, and they agreed to buy adjoining tracts and to establish a town in which they would be co-proprietors.

Rumsey was born in Sharon, Connecticut, on November 24, 1785, and, after his marriage to Olive Churchill, lived at Bethany, New York. According to a Rumsey genealogy he was accused of deserting his family in New York, and running away to Canada with a young "grass widow" named Mary Ann Sprague. A second charge involves some $3,000 that a company in Albany had loaned him to buy cattle. After he and Mary Ann left Canada for Michigan, they were discovered by a New York lawyer and taken back to Albany where he "suceeded in settling the charges against him." Rumsey's first wife had died on August 1, 1820, and the five children he left behind when he first departed with Mary Ann Sprague ranged in age from nine years to less-than-a-year. After the charges were settled he married Mary Ann sometime in 1823, sold the farm in Genessee County, New York, and returned to Michigan. The children were raised by relatives in New York. When John met them in Detroit early in 1824, Mrs. Rumsey was expecting a baby before spring.

Allen and Rumsey apparently spent some time in Detroit gaining the advice of the area businessmen and politicians. John also received several letters mailed to him in care of "Col. Smith" who may have been his host in Detroit. Although there had been missionaries and fur traders in Michigan since the late 1600's and settlement at Detroit for more than a century, the interior of the country was little explored. Government surveyors, sent to Michigan to locate land which could be awarded service veterans reported that the area was "one vast swamp" and "not more than one acre in a hundred, or perhaps a thousand, would admit of cultivation." Settlers beginning to fan out from Detroit were finding that the government report was a gross exaggeration, but the smart settler chose carefully after an on-site inspection.

Allen and Rumsey determined to look

at land in Washtenaw County, directly west from Wayne County where Detroit was located. The county had been created along with five others by proclamation of Lewis Cass, governor of Michigan Territory, on September 10, 1822, "to hold out inducements to migration and enterprize." The name Washtenaw was derived from a similar sounding Indian word which means, "the farther district," or "the land beyond."

The first settlement in the county occurred in the spring of 1823 when Benjamin Woodruff, formerly of Sandusky, Ohio, followed the Indian path known as the Sauk Trail that crossed lower Michigan to a townsite he called Woodruff's Grove, later the nucleus of the City of Ypsilanti. One of the early settlers at Woodruff's Grove, John Bryan, in an 1854 article of recollections wrote that on February 1, 1824, he had started walking from his cabin to Detroit through unbroken snow about six inches deep, "When about half way through the woods, I met two men in a one-horse sleigh. After enquiring if I thought they could reach the settlement before dark, they said they were going to find a place for a future home, and asked many questions about the country. They proved to be Messrs. Allen and Rumsey, who afterwards were the founders of Ann Arbor."

By February 12 they were at the Detroit land office where Allen purchased 480 acres, and Rumsey bought 160 acres of burr oak plain along the Huron River valley, in section 29, town 25, range six east, about ten miles west

The Ann Arbor plat filed in 1824

of Woodruff's Grove, and nearly 30 miles west from Detroit. The land they chose was in rolling country, the low hills broken by the Huron river valley. The original site was not on the river, but one corner of the settlement touched a small creek to the west. This stream, which they called Allen's Creek, was where they hoped to get fresh water for the town, and water power for its industries. Each proprietor paid cash for his land at the rate of $1.25 an acre, Allen, $600 and Rumsey, $200. The official patent when it came was signed by President James Monroe.

Promotion began immediately. On February 14, only two days later, Gov. Cass appointed a committee "to explore the County of Washtenaw and to establish the County seat thereof," and indicated that he had recently received an application from persons "interested in the County for the establishment of the County seat." Cass also recommended that the site chosen be on private property, "the location upon publick land would only excite an improper competition for procuring it."

Despite inclement weather, which the commissioners admitted in their report restricted their travel, the committee set quickly about the task. John Bryan wrote later about meeting the group as he was walking back to Woodruff's Grove from Detroit. "They were on horseback; all were dressed in Indian blanket over-coats, and had their pantaloons seated and faced down in front with buckskin. Each had a tin cup. On enquiring, "What news?" James McCloskey, Esq., who knew me, replied that they had located the county seat on land recently purchased by Allen and Rumsey, about 10 miles up the Huron from our settlement." Bryan, when he recorded his memories of the day 25 years later, said it was easy to be certain of the date, because his son, Alpha Washtenaw Bryan (the first white child born in the county, hence the name) had been born on February 27, and he received the first news of the event from the commissioners.

The commissioners in their report to the governor, printed in the March 26, 1824 edition of the Detroit Gazette, said that the directive by the governor to locate the county seat on lands already purchased from the government "gave rise to apprehension (knowing as we did, that comparatively few tracts were owned by individuals) that our labors might be aborted." But they were soon satisfied that "the judgment and foresight of enterprising individuals who had become pioneers of that part of the country had enabled them to make selections which were inferior to none in the county."

"The interests of the county will best be promoted," the report continued, "by establishing the county seat on the south bank of the Huron of Lake Erie, which passes in a south-eastern direction, near the centre of the county upon lands owned by Allen and Rumsey, Esquires, vis. on the northeast quarter of section numbered twenty- nine. . . under a stipulation that Messrs. Allen and Rumsey contribute to the county in cash, in labor and materials toward the erection of the court house and gaol, and in the erection of a substantial bridge over the Huron, the amount of one thousand dollars, and that they further give to the county such lots and parcels of ground as the undersigned have deemed necessary for public uses."

The commission report concluded, "Messrs Allen and Rumsey, who but a few weeks since made their purchase, and who have since become the proprietors of the county seat, have already, under almost every disadvantage, erected a good frame house, are commencing large improvements, and have contributed liberally for the benefit of the public."

In the middle of all of this industry, Mary Ann Rumsey gave birth, some time in February to her expected child at Woodruff's Grove, probably with the assistance of Mrs. Woodruff, who often served in the capacity of midwife for women in the county. The baby, if it was born alive, lived but a short time.

In 1821 a territorial law made it mandatory for the proprietors of any new town to "cause a true map or plat thereby to be recorded" before any lots could be offered for sale. Allen and Rumsey filed such a plat in the Detroit land office "this 25th day of May A.D. at seven of the clock P.M." The main east-west street of the town was designated Huron Street, with Allen's land to the north, and Rumsey's to the south. Three streets on Allen's side which ran parallel to Huron were Ann (named for his wife), Catherine (probably named for his daughter whose first two names were Elizabeth May, but who often wrote her full name, Elizabeth M. C. Allen), and North Street. The three major streets on Rumsey's side were Washington, Liberty and William. The five major north-south streets were numbered First through Fifth, but Third Street was also called Main. Allen set aside a square block on his side of Huron, between Main and Fourth Streets, as a public square for the court house. Rumsey donated one-half of a block on Liberty, between Fourth and Fifth for the jail.

If John had not yet made contact with his family he was busy writing to others. A. Bryant of Buffalo wrote in a letter dated March 5, 1824: "I am glad that you have fine Springs of water, and the sugar maple in your place, and plenty of fine fish, and that you have begun so early with an orchard." The orchard was the idea of Micajah T. Williams of Toledo, who stressed the usefulness of the fruit, along with the better appearance fruit trees give the village to prospective settlers. Bryant also alerted Allen to a Mrs. Taylor who was coming to his new settlement.

On April 28 he penned a second letter to tell John: "The boat starts tomorrow on her first trip. I have put your two boxes on board directed to Col. Smith in Detroit, as you directed me in your first letter, I have not paid any freight. Have not been able to sell the platter at any price, there will be some opportunity of accounting to you for it when I sell it, I have no charge against you except a little carting of the boxes." This would indicate that Allen left Virginia with at least two boxes of goods, or belongings of some type, and leads to speculation that "the platter" might have been household goods or a wedding gift that Allen was hoping to sell to finance his plans. Some goods had also been given to the Mission at Christmas.

On February 7, 1824, a suit was filed in Virginia in Augusta County Chancery Court by James Allen against his son, John Allen, and a list of people who owed John money. In reading the court files there seems from the language to be nothing malicious in the suit, it was simply a response by the elder Allen to his many creditors. In the brief filed his lawyer reiterates the failed efforts of John and William, and then of John alone, to settle their father's out-standing debts, and enters as evidence the letter that John wrote his father before he signed the debts and the property back to him. The file contains also a list of debts owed by John for which his father had stood security, including a $1750 bond to James Breckenridge, due in 1823.

"The said John has lately departed from Virginia and it is not probable that he will return," the brief continues, and includes a list of people who owed John money, describes two pieces of real estate he owned (1600 acres in Kentucky which was part of his first wife's inheritance, and 150 acres bought of William Bell), and points out other sources for possible garnishment, including the tenant on the 150 acres in

Augusta County who owed some rent, money due from James A. McCue for some real estate rented out, and "a crop of wheat and rye sown by the said John Allen before his departure."

It would appear that the intent of the suit was to throw James Allen's botched financial affairs into the judicial process and let the courts sort it out. This was essentially the outcome, although the final decision on the case was not rendered until 1825. By the tax roll of 1825 the land formerly owned and occupied by James and John Allen, had been divided and the new owners listed as George Baylor, William Bell and John Johnston, although Col. James had managed to reserve his right of residence until October of 1824.

There was apparently a good deal of animosity toward John in Augusta County. On the tax roll of 1824, he is listed as the owner of both the 150 acre tract he had purchased from William Bell, and the 500 acres that had been his father's. In the space in the tax roll book for

"	Gabriel		"
Alexander			"J"
Allen	John		Absconded
	"		
Allen	James	Colo	"
			Augusta
"			"

A portion of the 1824 tax roll

30

residence of owner, the tax collector had neatly penned "absconded." The 1825 tax roll gives John's address as "Michigan."

In 1825 in a letter to his aunt, Jane Trimble, he wrote: "You are the only one of my friends that has ex-pressed (in any form) an interest in my welfare, but am looked upon as unworthy a moment's thought, then have to regret that such a being was even born. Well I plead guilty -- for having left my family to suffer persecutions unheard of -- but as to my having the most distant idea of defrauding anyone, of their just rights I deny it with uplifted hands in the presence of a heartsearching God -- and was it not, my dear Aunt, that I have assurance in my own heart the one who seest and knowest all things and knowest the intention of his creatures, and judgest not as man judgest, I could not bear up under the loss of reputation and everything that a social being sets a value on -- I also feel confident (by the blessings of Providence) that the day is not far distant when I shall be able to prove to the world that I only detain from them a few pence to enable me to pay them the pounds."

It is not certain when John notified his family of his whereabouts, and that he was alive and safe. It was apparently not until summer that he wrote to them, giving directions and asking that they join him on the Michigan frontier. Aunt Jane Trimble whose home at that time was in Hillsboro, Ohio, was visiting the family of her daughter, Margaret, wife of James A. McCue, in Virginia, and wrote to her son in Ohio on August 20, 1824, that her brother Col. James Allen had visited the McCue house "yesterday with a letter to Ann; he has one from John Allen directing him what way to go & insists on his not coming without Ann, as he cannot live without her; her friends are all opposed to her going."

J. Marshall McCue later described the scene: "I remember, as an urchin of eight or nine, the assemblage at our house, of Maj. William Bell, brother-in-law, of my two grandmothers, sisters Jane and Betsy, of this Col. James Allen, with Uncles John and Franklin McCue, Uncle Andrew Barry, and my grandmother Jane Trimble, there on a visit. . . to consult as to the propriety of Aunt Ann, with her infant, Sarah. . . accompanying her father-in-law and family to Michigan in the county of Washtenaw. After praying over it for 24, 36, or 48 hours, can't remember the time, it was decided she had better go." Ann's two sons by her first marriage, both still under the age of 10, were not permitted to accompany her. They remained at the home of their guardian in Virginia.

If the dates are accurate, it was exactly a week later, August 28, 1824, that James and Elizabeth Allen, their youngest son James Turner Allen, then barely 20; eight-year-old James Crawford Allen, and five-year-old Elizabeth May Allen, John's children by his first wife; his second wife, Ann, and their sixteen-month-old daughter, Sarah Ann, and a young man named Orville Barnes who

32

had been teaching school in Virginia, left their home for the frontier of Michigan. Turner, who lived into his eighties, later recorded a detailed account of their journey. Actually, there are at least two different versions, all show the polishing of time and retelling, and present a fascinating story of travel in the early days of settlement. The account below covers the highlights of Turner's recollections:

We traveled all the way by land to Sandusky City which is situated on Lake Erie on Sandusky Bay in the State of Ohio. Our traveling out fit consisted of an old fashioned Pennsylvania Wagon (Covered) drawn by four horses, and three riding horses with saddles. The riding horses were a great Convenience for any of the party becoming fatigued or weary riding in the wagon, could relieve themselves by taking a ride on horseback. Not one of the party slept in a house during our long and tedious journey to Lake Erie. We had a good tent which we pitched every night, and which was occupied by all of our Company except Mr. Barnes and myself; our lodging place was in the wagon. . .

We left the Kanawha River at a point somewhere below the village of Charleston which is situated on said River and

took a road that passed
through what was called Tease
valley expecting to strike the
Ohio River some distance
below, where the Kanawha
empties into the Ohio River. .
. In passing through the
valley I think I never saw
such quantities, and such fine
peaches as I saw there. I
asked a man that appeared to
be the proprietor at that
place, if we could have some
of them; he said we were
welcome to all we wanted, and
might load our wagon with them
if we chose to do so. I
thanked him, and noticing a
large tree that had some large
rosy cheeked ones on it, from
that Mr. Barnes and myself
filled a bag. They were
clingstones, and proved to be
splendid. Mother would slice
them up, and fry them in Ham
gravy, and I think I never
tasted anything that I liked
any better. . .

In passing down the Ohio
or Kanawha River (I cannot now
recall to my remembrance
which) we crossed a river at
its mouth in a Ferry Boat that
emptied into one of the
Rivers, and after crossing the
stream the Bank being quite
high and steep and the ground
clayey, and the rain falling
at the time made the Road so
slippery that our horses
(being smooth shod) could not

34

pull the wagon up the bank; we
took a Pick or Mattock and dug
little trenches across the
road, to give the horses a
foothold, but then they could
not pull it up. While in this
dilemma, there was a Keel Boat
comeing down the River, and
Father beckoned to the Captain
of the Boat to come too; he
did so, and we put effects
aboard of the Boat, except
such as we would need on our
journey before we reached
Gallipolis, where the Captain
of the Boat was to have them;
he giving us the name of the
person there to whom he would
deliver them. After being
relieved of most of our load,
the horses pulled the wagon up
without much difficulty. When
we put our goods aboard of the
Boat, Father in our trouble
and hurry forgot to take the
name of the Captain or of the
Boat on which we put them; and
when we arrived at Gallipolis
we called on the person there
with whom the goods were to be
left, and making inquiry for
them, he asked the name of the
Captain to whom we had
entrusted the goods, not
knowing we could not give it
to him; he then asked the name
of the Boat, for the same
reason we could not give that
to him either. He then
intimated to us, that if we
had delivered our goods to the
Captain of one of the river

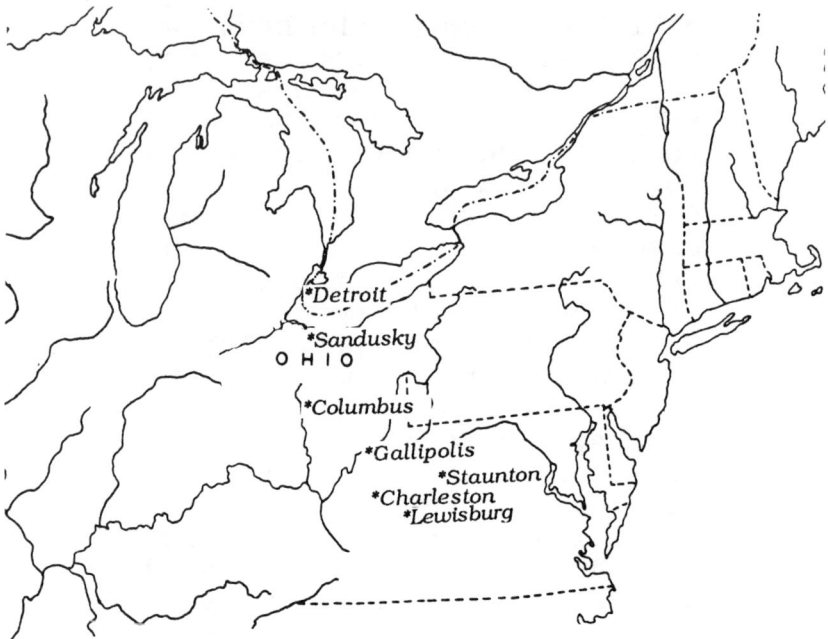

*Detroit

*Sandusky

O H I O

*Columbus

*Gallipolis

*Staunton
*Charleston
*Lewisburg

Keel Boats without taking a receipt for them, or knowing the name of the Captain or the Boat; the chances were against us of ever seeing them again, and that they were probably at that time a good many miles down the River. Father said he took the Captain of that Boat to be an honest man, and was loathe to believe that he was mistaken. After keeping us in Suspense some time he said to Father that he was not mistaken in the man, that he was honest, and that our goods were all safe in his warehouse, and that it was lucky for us that we happened to give them in charge of the person we did, that as a general thing the Captains on those Keel Boats were not any too honest. We felt pretty well after learning that our goods were all safe. We went to work and loaded them into the wagon and started on our journey through Ohio. . .

The northern part of Ohio that we passed through was at that time new and sparcely settled. We had heard that there was a Swamp which was called the black swamp, which extended some distance around the head of Lake Erie, and out into the Country, and through which we would have to pass if we continued our journey by land. . . We came to a place in the Wyandotte Indian reservation in Northern Ohio. Here we found ourselves right among the Indians; and from what we had heard and read of the Savage Character of the Indians we felt afraid of them. My Brother's wife said that their Cattle lowed Savage, and what added to our fears was, soon after our arrival at the place where we intended to camp for the night we saw an Indian mount a Pony and go off at a full gallop, as we surmised, to notify other Indians of our arrival and that they would come some time in the night and murder us, and appropriate what little property we had to their own use. But as there was no alternative for us; but to stay there, and take the chances, we unharnessed our horses; pitched our tent, built a fire and prepared our supper; after we had partaken of it Father thought he would reconnoiter around a little, and see how things appeared. He had only a short distance to go to the Indian cabins, (which had some appearance of civilization and comfort) and upon approaching one of them he heard the voice of someone. He proceeded cautiously, and there to his great surprise he saw an oldish Indian, perhaps a chief or one of their head men kneeling down before the mercy seat, lifting up his voice in prayer and supplication to the great all Father; in language unknown to him; but undoubtedly understood by him to whom it was addressed. When Father returned to our Camp he said we need not have any fears in regard to the Indians doing us any harm; he said while we were fearing the Indians they were fearing God.

We proceeded on our journey down the Sandusky River, through upper and lower Sandusky (at the former place there was a missionary establishment) to Sandusky City which is situated on Sandusky Bay Lake Erie. There we hoped to be able to ship

all on board (including our
wagon and horses) on the Steam
Boat Superior, she, then,
being the only Steam Boat on
the Lake. . . We waited for
several days, but to our great
disappointment when she did
make her appearance she passed
by the mouth of the Bay and
did not come into the Harbor.
So our hope of shipping our
horses to Detroit by water
failed. There was then in the
Harbor a Schooner called the
Hannah, the Captain of which
offered to take the family and
all our stuff aboard and take
them up to Detroit (except our
horses), and this being the
only chance we had, Father
made a bargain with him to do
so. We took our wagon apart
and shipped it with all of our
other articles (except our
tent, which was forgotten and
left on the Dock) and all of
our Company went on board;
except Mr. Barnes and myself,
we were elected to go through
the black swamp around the
head of Lake Erie with our
seven horses. . .

We arrived in Detroit
about Nine O clock that
evening (the fourth day).
Father had a man on the look
out for us; and soon after we
entered into the City, he
hailed us and found we were
the persons he was looking
for. He took us to the place

39

where the family was stopping; we found them all safe and well; and there we found Bro. John, he having previously arrived there from Ann Arbor. It was a happy meeting, and a time of rejoicing to us all, that we were again permitted to meet each other under circumstances so favorable. Father had the wagon put together, and our stuff all stowed away in it previous to our arrival, ready for a start for Ann Arbor which was about forty miles distant and over a verry bad road most of the way which we yet had to travel before our long and tedious journey would come to an end. We left Detroit the twelfth of thirteenth day of October, and arrived in Ann Arbor on the Sixteenth day of the same month A.D. one thousand eight hundred and twenty four.

The Hannah was a merchant sloop that had been built at Black Rock (later Tonawanda), New York, in 1816 for Charles Townsend, George Coit and Oliver Coit of Buffalo. Oliver Coit was master for many years. She was about 65 feet long and a little over 17 feet wide. In later years she was rerigged as a schooner and is probably the Hannah that was wrecked off Amherstburg, Ontario, in 1844. The Superior was the second steamboat on the Great Lakes, being the successor to Walk-In-The-Water, which was built in 1818 and lost in 1821. The Superior used the earlier boat's engines

and ran until 1833 when she was made
into a sailing craft, and her regular
service taken over by new, larger and
faster boats. Between 1822 and 1826 the
Superior was the only steamboat opera-
ting on the upper lakes.

Unlike many early travelers, the
Allens carried tents for shelter during
the journey. These were probably made
from cloth manufactured at the Staunton
textile mills. The mills were commis-
sioned during the Revolutionary War to
make "sail duck", fabric for use in the
construction of sails for the Virginia
fleet, and continued to be a major
manufacturer of heavy cloth for many
years. This same fabric was useful for
the construction of tents and other
shelters.

Ann Arbor

Probably because neither of the founders ever wrote on the subject, a particularly large number of fanciful stories have grown up around the naming of Allen and Rumsey's new settlement in Washtenaw County. No name was used by the commissioners when they chose it as a county seat in March of 1824. The first official use of the name, was on the plat of the village recorded by the Wayne County Register of Deeds on May 25, 1824, where it was written "Annarbour".

There is some evidence that other names were considered. A letter from William A. Moseley of Buffalo, written on April 29, 1824, in reply to a letter from Allen written during the previous February called the new settlement, "Allensville." In May, A. Bryant addressed his letter to John at "Anapolis, Michigan Territory."

There is little question that the name Ann Arbor was chosen by Rumsey and Allen to honor their wives, Ann Allen, and Mary Ann Rumsey. The arbor could have referred to an actual garden structure, or, more probably, spoke of the burr oak opening which several contemporary writers have suggested, "resembled an arbor." When the question came up once early in the twentieth century, the author who had written that the town was named for Mrs. Allen and Mrs. Rumsey received a forceful letter from a lady who was determined that three, not two,ladies by the name of Ann were being honored and that her aunt, Ann Scofield Hammond, was the third.

As recently as 1956 *Michigan History* published a fanciful but plausible tale by Lillian Dykstra, in which Rumsey and Allen discuss the subject. Perhaps the most outrageous unsubstantiated story is repeated in *Ann's Amazing Arbor* published by Alger Buell Crandell in 1965. This version involves a crew of surveyors, one "much addicted to fire water. who had his turn at making signs when the crew surveyed among the hills of Ann Arbor. He made the arrow by chopping off a short piece of sapling, splitting it down the center, sharpening one end for the arrow's point, and fastening it above the blaze in a tree. But it was not satisfactory, even to his companions. They laughed at his wild attempts around the night's campfire where he did his printing and made his markers with such sad results. . . At the corner of Main Street near West Huron where the trail made its sharp turn west to run down to the ford in the swampy creek, he hung the history making sign: "Ziss iss ann Arror."

In 1924, when the citizens of the city commemorated the centennial of settlement, a marker was erected on the south side of West Huron Street, which includes a brass plaque showing two ladies in pioneer dress seated on a bench in an arbor, and below the words: "Near this spot stood a rustic arbor covered with wild grape vines. Here Ann Allen and Ann Rumsey, the wives of John Allen and Elisha Walker Rumsey, met frequently for rest and recreation. The arbor was called "Anns' Arbor," and from it in honor of these pioneer women, the city received its name."

In the earliest days the name of the settlement was spelled and punctuated in various ways: Annarbour, Anarbour, Ann's Arbour, and Ann-Arbour, but as the Americanization of the English language continued, led by Noah Webster in his

The 1924 commemorative marker

famous dictionary, many English words with the construction "our" like labour, harbour and arbour, dropped the "u", and and the name of the city became offici- ally Ann Arbor. The 1838 *Gazetteer of the State of Michigan* spells it "Arbour" in the text but corrects it in an errata noting, "commonly written Ann Arbor."

TO THE PUBLIC.

THE subscribers invite the attention of EMI-GRANTS, particularly of *Mechanics* and *Artisans*, to the village of

ANN-ARBOUR,

The County-seat of the County of Washtenaw, pleasantly located on the Lower Huron

Ann-Arbour is in the heart of a rich and ra-pidly populating country, distant about thirty miles from Detroit. The village has been laid out into convenient lots, and the proprietors now offer them for sale on the most liberal terms, to persons desirous of permanently locating.

A map of the village may be seen at the of-fice of the Register of Wayne County in De-troit, or by application to the subscribers, at Ann-Arbour. It is expected that a road, to run direct from the county-seat to Detroit, will be surveyed and laid out in the course of the sum-mer.

The subscribers pledge themselves to facili-tate, as far as possible, the views of emigrants and others, who may visit the county, for the purpose of locating.

JOHN ALLEN,   } Proprie
ELISHA W. RUMSEY, } etors.

June 1 ,1824.   5y†

On June 1, 1824, Allen and Rumsey placed an advertisement in the *Detroit Gazette* addressed: "To the Public. The subscribers invite the attention of EMIGRANTS, particularly of *Mechanics* and *Artisans*, to the village of ANN-ARBOUR, the County-seat of the County of Washtenaw, pleasantly located on the lower Huron. *Ann-Arbour* Is in the heart of a rich and rapidly populating country, distant about thirty miles from Detroit. The village has been laid out into convenient lots, and the proprietors now offer them for sale on the most liberal terms, to persons desirous of permanently locating. . . " It was signed, "John Allen and Elisha W. Rumsey, Proprietors."

There is some evidence that John put off writing to his family back in Virginia until he was able to provide that "good home" that J. Marshall McCue, says he talked about in his first letter to them. John Geddes wrote later that he had visited Ann Arbor July 16, 1824: "We arrived in Ann Arbor before night. Ann Arbor then had one house, a sort of frame, one story high. There was an additional log block house, one story and a half high, no rafters nor roof on it. There was a tent north of the house. John Allen was putting up in the tent. Elisha W. Rumsey and wife occupied the house and entertained persons who came viewing land. It was headquarters. These beginnings were near a brook on Huron treet."

When the Allen family finally arrived from Virginia, all lived in the log block house, by then complete with rafters and roof. Some time before February of 1825 John's parents, Elizabeth and James (children by his first marriage), and his brother James Turner, had moved into a small cabin of their own. John later sold this lot to his father for a dollar.

In a letter to his aunt, Jane Trimble, written February 20, 1825, John described their new life: "Ann appears to enjoy herself better than I ever saw her, we live in a small log house with but one room down and one upstairs (or ladder rather), with a good fireplace and cooking stove by which Ann does the work of our family with care, and none to fret or put her out of temper. When the business of the day is through with, and we have seated ourselves around the fire, there is none to disturb us, we lye down and rise up contented and happy -- conscious that it is well pleasing in the sight of our maker to see his creatures enjoying the labour of their own hands. . . I hope and believe that we shall live happy and agreeable."

If John had hoped to escape his creditors by moving to Michigan he did not elude them long. There is preserved in the William Woodbridge papers a letter dated May 17, 1824 and addressed to "Hon. Gabriel Richard, Delegate of Congress, Washington D.C." A Roman Catholic priest-missionary from France, and an influential citizen of Detroit, Father Richard was then serving as delegate from the Michigan Territory to the United States Congress. The letter was written by John Floyd of Washington, and stated that he had received a note on John Allen from General James Breckenridge of Botetourt County, Virginia. Floyd asked that Father Richard take the note to Detroit and "place it in the hands of some attorney for collection -- and inform General Breckenridge and communicate with him from time to time. . . Mr. John Allen formerly lived in Augusta Co., Virginia, and left that country about two years ago, or perhaps a little more, and is believed to be now settled on Huron

47

river about twenty miles from Detroit."
Floyd is wrong about the time that John
had been absent from Virginia, but as
the note to Breckenridge was over $1000
and was due in 1823, it is likely that
John was not very visible for some time
prior to his departure. The note was
apparently brought back to Michigan by
Father Richard and turned over to
William Woodbridge, then a Detroit
attorney, later governor of Michigan,
for collection. Whether he was ever
successful is not recorded. As late as
1827 there is a letter from him to John
urging that some action be taken on the
Breckenridge note.

There was a second blow in the year
1824 to John Allen's new-found happiness
and economic security. John Harford
arrived from the State of New York, and
representing himself as one of the men
instrumental in the building of Rochester, New York, he impressed on Allen how
important it was for the new settlement
in Michigan to have a good reputation
with influential businessmen in New York
State. John explained later to Attorney
William Woodbridge as the two planned a
case more than a decade later, Harford
wanted " to purchase all or part of the
property owned by Elisha W. Rumsey and
myself." Rumsey would not listen to his
scheme, so Harford continued with John
alone. "He said," John wrote, "that if I
would give him the one half of my
property as a matter of speculation that
the balance would in a few years be
worth more money than the whole would
have been had I kept it.

"I was but a short time from my

native state Virginia, had but little acquaintance with business or with human nature, and never being deceived by man, I swallowed all that Harford said," John wrote sadly later. Under shady circumstances (Harford insisted that no security be offered, and that the terms of the contract not be revealed for two weeks following its completion), he closed a contract with Harford transferring half of the village lots (with some specific exceptions), and all of the mill property, for the payment of some cash and the promise to built up-to-date mills (like those in Rochester) and a store. Harford brought in about $200 worth of goods, ran a store of sorts for a few weeks in the summer of 1824, and then vanished. John, thinking the contract was then void, sold a portion of the mill property to George Noyes. In the fall of 1825 Harford returned and renewed his claim to the property.

One of the people that John later asked for testimony was Titus Bronson, later the founder of the settlement of Bronson (which would become the City of Kalamazoo) who according to his written deposition, "in the latter part of the summer or early in the fall of 1824 was living in the family of John Allen in Ann Arbor, Michigan Territory." In his testimony Bronson corroborates some of the statements that Harford made concerning his "prominence" in New York State, and the profits Allen could expect if he entered into the deal. (Titus Bronson was one of the earliest land owners in Washtenaw County purchasing land in the spring of 1823, and additional acreage in July, prior to the arrival of Allen and Rumsey. In the fall of 1824 as Ann Arbor began a period of rapid development, he grew tired of living so close to town, and traded his 160 acres adjacent to the settlement to John Allen for a tract in section 17. According to John Geddes Bronson was in and out of Ann Arbor several times between 1824 and 1827.)

As native Virginians, the Allens were unusual on the Michigan frontier scene. Most of the state, at that time was being peopled by settlers from the east, especially New York State, although all of the New England states were represented as well. Many of these settlers were knowledgeable frontiersmen having paused for varying lengths of time in Ohio and Indiana. Contemporary Virginia writers, however, draw an important distinction between the population of the state east of the Blue Ridge Mountains, who tended to be the more aristocratic, moneyed, people of English background; and those west of the Blue Ridge Mountains (where Augusta County was located), who were more likely to be of Scottish or Irish stock, to have less inherited wealth, and where society tended to be less "Southern genteel" and more "frontier."

No record still exists that John, or any of the Allens, in any way acted "southern", or even that their speech betrayed their origins. (A granddaughter of Ann Allen, wrote later that her grandmother had a Scotch accent. She always said "me own" and spoke of her dress as "me frock.") However, an amusing, north-south story was told by Turner, in reference to their trip north: "When we left Detroit for Ann Arbor Mother and myself rode in a Buggy (one I think Bro. John came in from Ann Arbor) and in those days there were but few streams that were fordable that had bridges over them, when we came to the River Rouge in fording it we found the water quite deep, and the bank where we had to go out being quite high and steep, when we came to it our horse refused to pull us up. The Buggy being in the River and partly on the bank, I could not get out of the Buggy without getting into the water; I was about to try what virtue there would be in the whip when Bro. John called to me, saying hold on, that is a Yankee horse and it would not do to whip him, said we would have to coax him. He came down the bank, talked to him and patted him and stroked him on the nose, and after doing so a little while, he took him by the bridle and said "come along now, if you don't I won't give you any punkin Pie to-night," and the little fellow started, and took us up the bank as nice as could be. That took me down, being about the first Yankee performance I had seen."

On December 30, 1824, John Allen was appointed the first postmaster of Ann Arbour. For at least a period of time during his tenure as postmaster he seems to have been responsible for carrying the mail as well, and was frequently in trouble with the authorities. "Complaint has been made," the postmaster general's office wrote in June of 1827, "that you open packets addressed to the Ypsilanti post office in violation of your oath and instruction. In one instance, the post master of that office saw you deliver a letter to Mr. Leonard Muller, which was addressed to the Ypsilanti post office, and Mr. Powers alleges that you have frequently committed this irregularity. The Postmaster requires a satisfactory explanation. . ." But the postal customers of Ann Arbor sent "an exposition and several testimonials" in his favor and the Postmaster General was "satisfied."

Among the early bills made out to the firm of Allen and Rumsey one from a Detroit merchant paid April 1, 1824, during their earliest pioneering days included charges for salt, two tin cups, one teapot, blankets, nails, clover, flax and barley seeds, and two papers of "garden seeds". Turner relates that in the early days, before the court house was completed, the family used the court house square as a vegetable garden. At the time of their arrival John already had fifteen or more acres plowed and fenced north of Huron Street and east of Main Street. In 1825 the elder Allens planted about ten acres of the land north of the square in corn, and, according to Turner, "raised a first rate crop. We had about five hundred bushels as nice corn as anyone could desire to see, one half of which we gave to Bro. John for the use of the land. Our part proved to be a great help to us, as what little money we had left after our arrival at Ann Arbor was gone, and we had to rely upon our own labor to procure the necessities of life."

The settlement continued to grow.

The earliest-known picture of Ann Arbor drawn in 1853.

John wrote in February of 1825: "It is now twelve months since I settled here when there was not an inhabitant within ten miles, -- how different is the scene now, in the village and neighborhood there is between thirty and forty families, many of who are of the first respectability, roads have been opened in various directions, mills of every kind started, tradesmen putting their shops in operation, by way of preparation for the flood of emigrants that is expected next summer farmers busily engaged in fencing farms which nature has provided already cleared for them -- in short it already bears the appearance of an old settled country,

53

except the want of houses and barns."

Bethuel Farrand who arrived in the autumn of 1825 wrote later that he found 26 families in the upper town, eight log dwellings and one small frame house and a store with about $200 of merchandise. "In 1826 the population increased very rapidly," Farrand said, "but most of the emigrants though highly respectable, and many of them well-educated, were poor."

Although he owned a number of slaves at least as late as 1820, John Allen was apparently opposed to the institution. In 1826, he received from his brother-in-law Charles Lewis, comments that would seem to be in response to a letter from him: "It affords me a great deal of satisfaction to know that you are so well pleased with your situation; you have the richest soil, a facility to a good market, the climate excellent, and you are excepted from the curse of holding a portion of the human race in bondage. That slavery is an evil of great magnitude we are fully sensible."

"Oh, how great a curse are we delivered from" John wrote in 1825. "The thought of which at all times constrains me to bless and praise the disposer of all events, for thus delivering us; by a strong hand from a land of oppression and Tyranny, and placing us in a land of liberty and peace. . . "

As settlers purchased lands, John's investment began to make enough money for him to pay off several of the Virginia debts, although there was apparently never an effort made to redeem the land in the south. One tack he tried, with some success, was to use Michigan land as security for some of the Virginia debts, but there were some problems: "I think the plan you propose of securing your debt in this county, by a Deed of Trust upon real estate a good one," William Bell wrote from Virginia in 1825, "But I see some difficulty attending, for which reason I have not spoken of the plan to any of your creditors. I do not know anyone in that country to receive the money when due."

Perhaps to make up for the land he had lost in the Harford deal, John purchased many lots back from settlers who bought land in Ann Arbor and then moved to other property, or decided to move farther west. Even with the apparent prosperity in August of 1826, he received a letter from C. C. Trowbridge of the Bank of Michigan regretting to inform him that "it became necessary for the Directors to put your note in suit."

Although he was later a leader in the establishment of the Temperance Organization in Washtenaw County, John Allen's application for a license to retail "strong or spirituous liquors" was the first point of business at the first session of the Washtenaw County Court held January 3, 1827, at the house of Erastus Priest, Judge Samuel E. Dexter, presiding. "The court being satisfied that said tavern was necessary for accommodation of travelors, ordered a license to be issued."

John was the first coroner in Washtenaw county, and ran for representative in the territorial legislature in November of 1827. He finished a poor fourth. Voting in the race was, Henry Rumsey, 101; Abel Millington, 74; Benjamin J. Woodruff, 62; and John Allen, 40.

James Allen, John's father, dove with enthusiasm into life in Michigan and managed a grinding mill for at least a season before teaming up with son Turner to build a sawmill along the Huron River. Turner wrote later, "After we got it running it did not prove a verry profitable investment, but left us in debt some hundreds of Dollars." The next project by the elder Allen was a boat to run between Rawson's Landing, about 14 miles from Ann Arbor on the Huron River, and Detroit. The vessel was designed to carry families and their goods that were moving into the country, and also various kinds of freight from Detroit. Apparently shortly after service was begun in April of 1826, the *Detroit Gazette* wrote: "This boat is of a different construction from any one that has been built here. It is 70 feet in length and seven in width, with a light draught of water, and will carry 100 barrels. I am informed that it is built on the plan of the James River boats of Virginia, which have been found best adapted to the navigation of rapid streams without much depth of water. . . There is no doubt that, with a slight improvement of the navigation, boats of this design may open a communication between Oakland and Washtenaw, a result offering many advantages to both counties."

"The roads being very bad between Ann Arbor and Detroit, he had all the business he could do," son Turner wrote later. In the summer of 1828 on a run east Col. Allen was taken ill ("the country at the mouth of the River and on the Lake (Erie) through which he had to pass being low and marshy," Turner explained), and he was just able to get home, dying seven or eight days later on July 18, 1828. His presence was sorely missed by both of his sons, and by the Ann Arbor community as well. They remembered him as a cheerful, white-haired man who played the fiddle on social occasions. Following his death, his widow and John's two children by his first marriage, James C. and Elizabeth, returned to Virginia where they lived with relatives for the next five years.

Another death, which was to affect the development of the settlement, was that of Elisha Walker Rumsey on September 5, 1827. Although he owned less land than Allen, he was active in the community, having been appointed a justice of the peace and named a captain in the local militia. His widow married William Van Fossen, an early settler in Jackson County. In the mid-1830s the Van Fossens moved to Lafayette, Indiana, where Mary Ann died of cholera in 1849.

The first teacher in the settlement was Orville Barnes, the young man who had come north with the Allen family in 1824. Although he instructed pupils he never held full-scale classes, mainly tutoring his young charges in their homes. In September of 1825, a schoolmarm named Monroe began conducting a primary school in a log building constructed by John Allen on his property on the northwest corner of Main and Ann Streets. Surely two of the first pupils were James C. Allen, then about ten, and his sister Elizabeth, eight. An incident was related in an 1852 article in *Godey's* written for Mrs. E. F. Ellert by Mary H. Clark of Ann Arbor concerning a time when James C. was a youngster and came home to report that the teacher could not continue her work because the daily walk from her home to the school was endangering her health. "He came running home, so out of breath he could not speak, and entreated his grandmother to take the teacher to live in her home. . . . After consulting with her husband she bade him 'Tell her she may come and take us as she finds us.' He ran back delighted and presently returned with the teacher, so grateful for the offer of a home which enabled her to continue her beloved occupation that, when the little boy led her in with, 'Grandmamma, here she is,' she sank upon a seat and wept for joy."

In later years John Allen lamented that his children had "but little education." (However, all three of his children could write a reasonably educated letter.) "To sustain yourself in respectable and well-bred company creditably," he wrote his son in 1836, "you must have a mind well stored with information on a variety of subjects, and possess what is termed, polished manners. Literature with awkwardness, or Riches with Vulgarity -- never will enable its possessor to more in good society. How rare in Michigan are young men of good breeding. . . Every man takes his stand in society just where his mind and manners entitle him. If you ever desire, or expect, to move in the first circle with credit to yourself, you will have to prepare for it."

John himself did not have extensive institutional learning. There is no evidence that he ever attended a college of any kind, but Rev. Lorenzo Davis, who knew him as early as 1828 recalled that he was "physically a very grand speciman of a man. He was over six feet tall and well proportioned. He was well educated, not a classic scholar, but a very good English scholar, and very apt in acquiring the elements of science and had a happy facility of properly appropriating what he possessed."

John Allen was instrumental in founding in 1829 a private school, later called the Ann Arbor Academy. A school for boys, it had a good reputation on the Michigan frontier, drawing students occasionally even from the Detroit area, most notably the young son of William Woodbridge.

It was about 1829, just as the Academy was getting under way, that John decided to take up the study of law. His troubles with the promoter Harford had demonstrated his deficiencies, and he was determined it would not happen again. In December of 1829 he received a list of Michigan Bar members from J. W. Torrey, and the advice that Torrey's law education had cost him a fee of $300, and that $150 of that sum had been written off because of "attention to the business of the office." Under similar terms John commenced study with James Kingsley, an early Ann Arbor attorney. In 1830 Kingsley was appointed Judge of Probate, an office he held until 1836. John Allen was named Justice of the Peace in 1830, and later acting Register of Deeds. By 1833 he had hung out a shingle in front of a little white building on Huron Street, where he carried on his real estate business, acted as notary, and took such law cases as came his way, mostly debt collection requests from out-of-town clients.

As early as 1828 John and his brother James Turner, had been partners in a store. The partnership was later dissolved and the *J. Kingsley* business known as James T. Allen and Company. John continued however to bring in quantities of books, stationery supplies, clothing, and yard goods from New York City for sale in Ann Arbor and to other Michigan merchants. These goods were usually purchased on credit, and were often followed several months later by letters that said, "We have written you several times respecting our a/c with you and confess we are disappointed in not hearing from you, not only because of our demand not being paid, but from the inattention you have shewn toward it," and "Sir: The acceptance you gave me payable at Detroit Bank came back protested, and I hear nothing from you on the subject.

When you gave me your <u>word of honor</u> I could do no less than accede to your request -- and I cannot now believe that some accident has prevented your compliance. . ."

To add to an already busy schedule in 1828 John took up the cause to make illegal the practice of Masonic orders. The question of secret societies was often a topic of controversy, being defended as a source for pleasure and fellowship by some, and loudly protested by others, including some of the leading churches. Anti-Masonry forces rallied after an incident in New York State in which a former member of the brotherhood announced that he was now opposed to the institution and would reveal its secrets. He disappeared shortly after that announcement. The issue grew until an Anti-Mason political party was formed. In 1828 John had apparently written to John P. Sheldon, owner of the *Detroit Gazette*, urging him to make his newspaper an exclusively Anti-Masonic newspaper. Sheldon replied in an indignant letter, August 19, 1828: "I will make no bargain, neither will I pledge the columns of the Gazette to the <u>exclusive</u> use of any party; for I hold, that in every public paper (whatever may be the modern practice) discussion should be free."

Allen, as part of a committee, ran an ad in the Gazette in July of 1829, addressed "To Printers: There is an excellent opportunity for the establishment of an Anti-Masonic Press in the village of Ann Arbor. . . " but got no takers, although several offered to sell him the equipment if he wished to run his own newspaper. In December of 1829, that is just what he did. Allen, along with Samuel W. Dexter, bought out Thomas Simpson, owner and founder of the *Western Emigrant*, the first newspaper published in Ann Arbor. In their first issue they promised a "vigorous opposition to Freemasonry", and as a result 80 readers cancelled their subscriptions.

Following the first issue Erastus Ingersoll wrote: "That you have succeeded in your exertions in establishing a press in your flourishing county is a source of much gratification to me particularly if it is, as I have no reason to doubt, a free press." After the second issue, E. P. Hastings penned: "I see you have become an editor. I wish you success in your arduous and responsible situation. . . " Ebenezer Reed who had been introduced as their Washington correspondent, commented by letter: "As to the appearance of your paper I like it well--the only fault I find is that it has too much anti-masonry--one column a week is enough in all conscience. Too much of any one thing is sure to beget satiety."

A second cause espoused by the new editors was temperance. After carrying articles concerning a new scientific process for distilling corn oil, and making other things from corn, the editors commented in the January 20, 1830, issue: "We are decidedly opposed to the practice of converting corn, or any other kind of grain, into the liquid poison (called whiskey) yet so far as this discovery tends to the advancement of the arts and science, we wish it success."

Dexter lived in the town that took his name eight miles northwest of Ann Arbor, and, his daughter wrote later, would head out for Ann Arbor where the paper was printed, once a week with his saddlebags stuffed with articles and correspondence. By mid 1830 Allen, busy with other tasks, had turned the leadership of the paper over to Dexter, George Corselius, and Mark Howard, Ann Arbor's first apprentice printer, although his name continued on the mast head until late in 1831.

One real problem, that threatened the prosperity of Allen's settlement, was a move by Anson Brown, founder of a competing settlement just north of the Huron River, to have the post office removed to his part of town. Brown attempted to enlist the assistance of Michigan politicians, in at least one case using "a few bottles of champaign" to convince them that as his part of town was growing faster, the post office ought to be moved there. This was done in 1833, much to the annoyance of the people on the hill who refused to go there for their mail, instead hiring neighborhood children to fetch it for them. Brown also campaigned for a territorial road that would enter Ann Arbor through the lower town, but he died in 1834 of cholera. Many feel that had he lived, the geographic development of Ann Arbor might have been changed.

Despite the complaints of his cre-ditors, it was a period of relative prosperity for John Allen. An 1830 insurance policy written by the New York Farmers' Fire Insurance and Loan Company reveals that he carried insurance of $1900 including: "$400 on a two story building of wood on the Public Square in the Village of Ann Arbor and occupied by Thomas M. Perry, printer of a newspaper in the second story and as a dwelling in the first story; $500 upon his two story building of wood situated on the corner of Main and Huron Streets and occupied by Colben Cornwill as a Tavern; $1000 upon his Two Story Building of Wood situated on the corner of Huron and Main Streets occupied as a Store, Law office and private dwelling." It is unclear in which of these buildings the Allen family resided.

The 1830 census for the only John Allen in Ann Arbor states that the household contained one male between the age of 5 and 10, a male and female between the ages of 30 and 40, and one male between the ages of 12 and 20. The youngest person in the census is surely a mistake, as the only individual under ten in the household was young Sarah Ann. The person between 12 and 20 was probably a servant.

The young person was definitely not either of John's children by his first marriage, who were still down in Virginia with their grandmother. James C., then a lad of 17, wrote in March of 1833: "I have seated myself to write you a few lines and to let you know where I am and what I am a doing. I am at Uncle Billy Bells a going to school to Mr. Alfred at present. Uncle Bell has been

64

very kind to me, if it had not of been for him I dont know what I would of done for clothing. I received a letter from you a few weeks ago. . . it gave me much gratification to know that you intend to send for us this spring. Dear Father do not neglect sending for us, I am almost crazy to get home. I think the most of the friends will be twice glad if they were glad when we came they will be glad when we go. I think they would be willing to keep Grandmother, but sister and myself must go. I feel sorry for sister, she has got no education and no way of getting any in this country depending on our friends." The following summer James, Elizabeth, and their grandmother returned to Ann Arbor with other relatives.

The settlement of Ann Arbor was incorporated as a village in 1833, and at the organizational meeting John Allen was elected its first president. The meeting was held at the inn of Chauncey S. Goodrich on Fourth Avenue. The council was called upon to decide such important questions as who would have the annual privilege of farming the meadow below the business district. The custom was to lease it to the highest bidder. It was during John's tenure as village president that the first county court house was erected in Ann Arbor. The cornerstone was laid June 19, 1833, on the land John had given. The building faced south and stood close to the Ann Street line leaving the remainder of the block a fenced public square. There were three doors in the front, the middle one opening into a hallway which ran the length of the structure, exiting at the opposite end. On either side of this hall were rooms which were rented to lawyers for offices. The court room was on the second floor. When court was not in session it was used for public gatherings and entertainments of all kinds. On the south roof peak was a small hexagonal cupola. The main building was flanked by two one-story annexes, one for the register of deeds, one for the county clerk. (This complex served Washtenaw County until 1878 when a new brick and granite structure was built in the center of the square. The 1878 building was replaced in 1955.)

Also in 1833 John Allen teamed with

The first Washtenaw County Courthouse

Lovett Eames to establish a water service, (to cost private houses $8 a year, public houses, $20), and be supplied from a spring on the Allen farm, to be delivered at the front door of each subscriber "as early in the day. . . as will be practicable." Patrons had to sign a contract promising not to let others use their water, and not to draw or use any water except for "drinking, cooking, washing and scrubbing in the household arrangement."

Fresh from a term as president of Ann Arbor, Allen ran in April of 1835 as a Federalist to serve as delegate to a constitutional convention to draft the document that would govern the new State of Michigan. Not only did all the Federalist candidates lose to the 15 Democrats, but John Allen was the third lowest vote getter among the 15 Federalists.

His financial problems did not abate. When he was not using his new understanding of the law to foreclose on others, he was defending suits against his own overdue debts. There is also some undercurrent that all is not well on the home front. In March of 1835, the *Ann Arbor Argus*, reviewing the candidates for the election said of John Allen: "Men, freemen of Washtenaw. Do you regard domestic peace and happiness? Do you care ought for those virtues which endear and render private life happy? Let your vote answer." Also in August of 1836, John in writing to James C. who was attending school in New York state studying to be a surveyor, said:

"We found Grandmother, Sarah, Thomas and all your friends and acquaintances well. Mother is now alone and says she enjoys herself well. Sarah Ann has almost grown out of my knowledge." It was about this time that John was often gone for weeks, and sometimes months at a time, tending to projects farther west, leaving the womenfolk back in Ann Arbor. It is uncertain what comment this situation makes about domestic tranquility in the marriage, or in the home situation.

Thomas McCue, Ann's son by her first marriage, having reached the age of majority, was apparently visiting when the above was written. He and his brother John had been cared for by their uncle's family in Virginia in accordance with the will left by their father. The uncle was also responsible for handling the McCue estate which included both assets and debts. A meticulous account was filed in Augusta County Circuit Court August 29, 1839, giving a year-by-year record. This included money raised by hiring out a number of slaves that had been left to the boys by Dr. McCue, and rent on some of their real estate. When each reached the age of majority they were given sufficient money to permit them to visit their mother in Michigan.

Ann Arbor was well-launched by 1835 and John Allen was ready to turn to new adventure. To yet unpeopled wilderness, where there were streams and rivers flowing free, mills to be built, and post offices yet to open.

Van Buren County

If the nation's economy had given John Allen's dreams a chance, Van Buren County today would have two thriving cities of Mason and Middletown, and South Haven would have come into its own as a commercial center two decades earlier.

Moving directly west from Ann Arbor Allen went past Kalamazoo, (then known as Bronson, and settled by his old friend Titus Bronson), and into the next row of counties which had been formed in 1829. This area was just opening to settlement. The name of John Allen is on the land records as an early purchaser of cheap government land. He also bought acreage from the original purchaser in most of the townships in the county. (Government land had to be paid for in cash at the time of purchase; it was often possible to purchase from others with easier terms.)

Mason

In June of 1835 John Allen bought 40 acres in the southwest quarter of the northwest quarter of section 10 in the township later called Lawrence. The settlement had a geographical configuration that seemed to be John's preference in nearly all of his ventures. It was located on a small stream (Brush Creek) near its confluence with a larger river (Paw Paw River). He called it Mason, in honor of the then-governor of Michigan Territory, Stevens T. Mason.

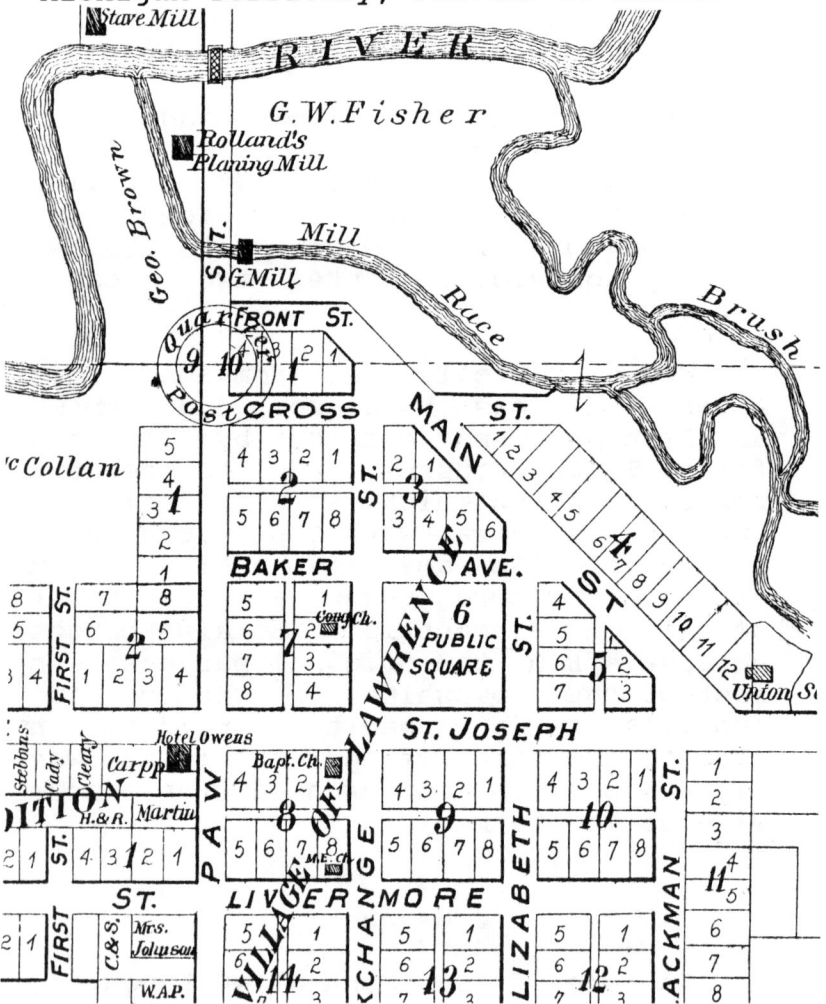

An 1895 map of downtown Lawrence.

According to a story later recounted in an 1880 county history: "Having laid out his town on paper, Mr. Allen, who had himself no intention of actually settling, looked about him for some man whom he could induce to begin the improvement of the place. He interviewed Eaton Branch of Ann Arbor, upon the matter; but Branch was not inclined toward the venture. Shortly afterwards Allen met Branch saying, "I don't want you; I've got a man and his wife to go out to Mason." "Who's the man," asked Branch. "Ephraim Palmer." "Ephraim Palmer?" replied Branch; "well, all I have to say to you is, watch him." "Oh," retorted Allen, "you needn't attempt to set me against Palmer; I am a phrenologist, I tell you, and I am thoroughly satisfied that the man is honest." So Palmer and his wife, fresh from Ohio, went to Mason, and from a spot on the bank of Brush Creek, about thirty-five rods north of the Lawrence school-house, he cleared the underbrush preparatory to putting up a log cabin. It was in August, 1835, that the Palmers reached the place. . . he cut logs of fourteen feet in length for his house and when he was ready to raise it he had the assistance of Allen, Fountain, E. Barnum (who had just come in from Paw Paw), and a man who happened to be there in search of land. . . About a month after Palmer's settlement he left the place suddenly and was heard of no more, except that he passed through St. Joseph, with his wife, on their way West. It is said that his sudden departure caused Mr. Allen to lose faith in the value of his phrenological knowledge."

(The wonder is that John Allen ever had any faith in phrenology. An undated manuscript in the Burton Historical Collection titled "Phenological Character of John Allen, Ann Arbor", includes the information that he is "not over anxious for property or wealth," and "Fond of home, and no desire for roving about." The analysis was a little more accurate in the statements that he was "not marvelous about strange things," and possessed "large hope." Phrenology, the pseudo-science of determining the characteristics of an individual by examining and measuring the shape of the head, was popular in the nineteenth century.)

During his short stay in Lawrence Palmer figured in another story later recorded in a county history. After he and his wife were settled in their new cabin one day Edwin Barnum, the surveyor, John Allen and his son, James C., paid a visit. "Supplies were all out, and Palmer started for Kalamazoo for a stock, but a fearful rain-storm coming on, the country was flooded, and he was six days making the trip. Meanwhile the Allens, Barnum, and Mrs. Palmer subsisted on cranberries and coffee. Allen caught a woodchuck, but there was no salt in the house, and the project of cooking it was about to be abandoned, when a few wild leeks being found, they were forced to do duty as seasoning, although the dish was voted distasteful, despite the hunger of the party."

Not long after Ephraim Palmer's departure the cabin was occupied by John Reynolds. According to the 1880 history "On November 15, 1835, Reynolds and his wife received into their cabin a delegation of eleven people, ten of whom came to settle, and as Reynolds' house was the only one at hand, they were forced to crowd into it. These people were Eaton Branch and wife, Dexter Gibbs and wife with five children, John Allen, and William Williams. There were thirteen, all told, who occupied the house, and as the room in which they slept was but twelve feet square they were really in close quarters. As a matter of convenience, the gentlemen selected for their dressing-room an out-door spot behind a brush pile."

Eaton Branch, a native of Vermont, came to Michigan about 1825, stopping first in Ann Arbor. He was married in 1833 to Amanda Melvina Allen (not related to John Allen's family) and moved to the new settlement of Mason in 1836 to assist in the clearing of land and building of roads. His son, Ira, was the first white child born in what would later be Lawrence, according to a family genealogy. His mother and father, Vine and Abigail (Eaton) Branch, and two brothers, Israel and Luther, were also residents of Lawrence before 1840.

John Reynolds had come to Michigan with his father, and three brothers. He had been a boatman in Ohio, and for some time he was actively engaged in flat-boating on the Paw Paw River between Lawrence and St. Joseph. When the railroad replaced water transportation,

Reynolds, left Lawrence and opened a bakery in Paw Paw.

The congestion at the cabin lessened after John Allen built a double log house nearby. On the ground floor were two rooms each 14 feet square with sleeping apartments above. One end of the ground floor was later used as a tavern. Dexter Gibbs was proprietor, until his death October of 1838.

In 1836 John Allen and John R. Haynes built a saw mill finally getting it in operation in early winter. In 1838 a grist mill was added to the structure. Haynes was later postmaster, the second coroner in Van Buren County, and one of the associate judges of the county court. He continued to serve the community as merchant and miller until his death in 1856.

It frequently occurred in Michigan that there was some delay between the formation of a county and its actual organization. Van Buren County was formed in 1829, but it did not begin to function as a county until 1838. It spent the intervening years designating county seats. The first county seat in the official territorial records was located by a commission and designated by George B. Porter, governor of Michigan Territory in May of 1833. It was described as " a point on the east line of section one three chains from the quarterstake in town three south of range fifteen west and within about 20 rods of the head of navigation of the Paw Paw River," (this would be in the northeast corner of what was later

Lawrence Township) and for the privilege its proprietors were to pay $1,000, and give land and $100 toward the erection of a court house. In 1835, about the time Allen came on the scene, a new commission selected a site within the present village of Lawrence, then John Allen's settlement of Mason, as "the proper place for the county seat." Eaton Branch said the commissioners stuck the stake designating the site of the court house in the center of the public square. In March of 1836 a second law was passed, reconfirming the action of the commission in selecting a site but added the provision that the proprietors of the site "shall pay into the treasury of this State the amount advanced from the Territorial treasury for said location, with interest thereon from the date of such advance." But when the county was actually organized in 1837 the weight of population had shifted to Paw Paw, and a petition was circulated to get the county seat moved to that village. This was officially done in 1840.

John appears to have lived in the settlement at Mason for a time. In January of 1836 he received a letter from Samuel Denton of Ann Arbor addressed: "John Allen, Allen, Van Buren County, M. T." (Allen was apparently one name that was considered for the new settlement. A land transfer dated December 13, 1835, for Eaton and Amanda Branch, identifies them as "both of Allen, Van Buren County". Witness to the deed was John Allen.) John's wife, Ann, remained in Ann Arbor and was visited in the summer of 1836 by Thomas and John

McCue, the sons from her first marriage who lived at the house of their guardian in Virginia. On September 6, 1836, Thomas wrote to his stepbrother James C., who was attending school in New York State: "Pa is now out west and has been nearly two weeks past but he is expected to return in about two weeks. We have not heard from him since he left." (There seems to have been a good relationship between all of the children in the family, Ann's sons Thomas and John McCue, John's children Elizabeth and James C. Allen, and the only child of their marriage, Sarah Ann Allen. All of the children called John and Ann, "Mother" and "Father," and referred to each other as "sister" and "brother" in their frequent letters.)

In 1836 John Allen had the government contract to carry the mails between Kalamazoo and St. Joseph, so he altered the route of the mail stage to veer through the settlement of Mason. In addition to the mail, the stage carried passengers and freight. The same year John undertook to build a road between Mason and St. Joseph. In April he received a contract from Lucius Abbott of St. Joseph agreeing to pay one hundred dollars toward building a road between his settlement on Brush Creek and the Paw Paw mills providing that the owners of the mills would do the same and "further provided that the said Col. Allen, does not purchase the undivided half of the property." It is unclear why the title "Colonel" was used, John had been appointed by Lewis Cass as a Captain in the militia, but he was probably not active at this time.

In a letter dated December 28, 1836, Jesse Smith of Smithville, New York, part owner of the Paw Paw river mills at what would later be Watervliet replied cautiously: "You say you will open and bridge the road from Brush Creek to the bend in the Paw Paw river, about half way from Brush Creek to our mills provided we will open and bridge the road thence to St. Joseph. I say to you promptly that we will open or cause the same to be done from the Bend on the river six miles East of our mills through to where it will naturally intersect the Territorial road leading from Bronson to the mouth of the St. Joseph and bridge the stream and make the road as good as possible as you will make the other part and will have it done immediately. I will write Mr. Moffat this day to commence it, and I hope and trust you will be equally prompt in opening the part you propose."

The road was promptly begun with Eaton Branch doing most of the work on Allen's part. The major portion of it was opened in 1837.

Speculation in lands was rampant in 1835 and 1836, and a landowner's largest hope for a quick profit was often a sale to a speculator, but even that market was getting jittery. E. P. Hastings of Detroit wrote John in April of 1835: "I sold my village lots for $70. Perhaps I have sold too low--I do not feel able to invest anymore funds in stocks and I know of no one here that is. Our people want to borrow all they can lay their hands on. . . "

By 1837 John was no longer living in Mason, and he had given up the mail route which was, at least, a source of some ready cash. April 21 of that year J. R. Haynes, his partner in the Mason mill wrote: "The cashier at the Kalamazoo bank says there are no funds--and now insists on my paying the check. . . This is not as it should be. I want you to help me out immediately for I have not got the funds and cannot raise them at present. . . Our mill has been stopped about four weeks with the back water, but is now doing pretty fair business. We have on hand a good lot of lumber. Sales rather dull at present for money is scarce and hard to be got and unless you can let me have some of the needful, I shall be obliged to sacrifice property to keep out of the limbo."

But money for the project was not forthcoming and the settlement failed to grow much. By 1843 it still had less than a dozen families. The name Mason fell into disuse (mainly because of two other Michigan towns, one in Cass County and one in Ingham county also named Mason in honor of the governor) and the little cluster of cabins around the mill and store was known commonly as Brush Creek. In 1846 John R. Baker, a Paw Paw lawyer, foreclosed on a mortgage and had the settlement replatted. He called it Lawrence, taking the name of the township.

Middletown

In 1836 John Allen located a number of lots of land on Hog Creek, in

Hartford Township, west of Mason. He platted the land into lots calling it Middletown. Pioneer settler Luther Sutton later told the story of the village:

In 1836, Mr. Allen attempted to establish a stage route from Paw Paw to St. Joseph via Middletown and Waterford (Watervliet). Some five or six families who had gathered at Brush Creek, having heard of Middletown, supposed it to be quite a village, and some of the men of the settlement proposed to visit it. The company consisted of about half a dozen ragged men and as many barefooted boys; but one of the company, John Mellen, a Mohawk Dutchman, being rather destitute of clothing then the rest, felt a little ashamed to go near strangers when Humphrey Barnum offered to lend him a coat. Mellen accepted, and the company started out. . . They soon struck the hills and after going up and down for about half a mile, came to what seemed to be the last place in creation, being a deep hollow, about forty rods across. . . Climbing out of this they came to Mud Lake, and a little farther passed Sutton's Lake and came to the great Indian trail which passed through the country north and south from

Pokagon to Lake Michigan. . .A little west of this they crossed the town line. . . Working their way through brush, over logs, and across small streams, they reached Middletown Creek, and crossing it took a seat upon the bank. . . There the party partook of their lunch, when Barnum told Mellen he would show him the village, and going a few rods he introduced him to the public square and other imaginary localities and business places, and also to the leading settlers, which were none other than mosquitoes, and he thought they had made themselves acquainted at least with some of the family. The joke was relished by the whole company, and was the source of considerable sport for years afterwards.

There is no record that any lots in Middletown were ever sold, and by the mid-1840's Joseph Grant of Oswego, New York came into possession of the land by foreclosure. It was eventually sold as farm land. In 1844, a settlement was begun about a mile to the west, which later became the Village of Hartford.

Black River

Jay R. Monroe, a native of New Hampshire, came to Michigan in 1826, and in 1833 built the first house at South Haven at the mouth of the Black River,

*Grand Haven
KENT
OTTAWA
IONIA
CLINTON
SHIAWASSEE
GENESEE
LAPEER
ST. CLAIR

Lansing* *Meridian
ALLEGAN
BARRY
EATON
INGHAM
LIVINGSTON
OAKLAND
MACOMB
*Richmond

*South Haven
VAN BUREN
KALAMAZOO
CALHOUN
JACKSON
WASHTENAW
*Ann Arbor
WAYNE
Middletown*
*Mason
*Spring Arbor

BERRIEN
CASS
ST. JOSEPH
BRANCH
HILLSDALE
LENAWEE
MONROE

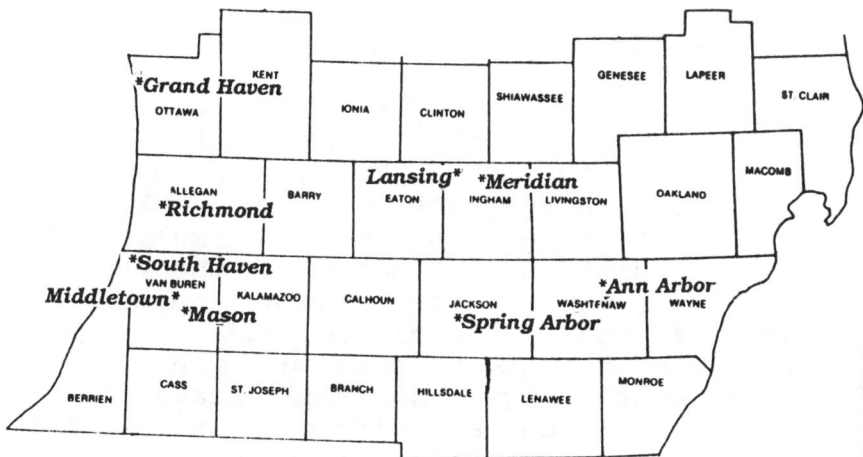

although he did not reside there. In 1837 he and his family moved to John Allen's settlement of Mason. In 1836 and 1837 village lots in South Haven, Van Buren County, were one of many land deals that John Allen offered his real estate customers, mostly investors in the east. Whether he actually owned these lands or served as agent for Jay Monroe, or for Jay's son Charles, who took over the land business, is uncertain. In June of 1837, when John was trying to cut a deal with Richard L. Lawrence and Joseph Hunt of Oswego, lots in the village of South Haven "not less than 29 by 100 feet" were going for one hundred dollars each.

The second South Haven area project was a mill to be built in partnership with Samuel Denton, on a branch of the Black River. Because of the size of the stream the immediate problem was low water. Denton advised Allen in a letter dated January 11, 1836, that he had made a bargain with Osterhout and White to build the mill, then added: "I have heard several modes of getting lumber down small streams spoken of lately. One is to take it down in flat boats from five to ten thousand feet at a time drawn by a horse walking on the bank. . . When the stream is too low a small dam can be built in the channel at the lower end. . . say two feet high at the sides and one foot in the middle, wide enough for the boat to pass through. In other cases a temporary wing will heave the water all in one side of the channel and by this means make it deep enough.

"We must if possible devise some means to get along without hauling. I hope you will have time to explore the stream thoroughly from one end to the other and also the harbor with reference to getting our lumber on board a schooner."

The mill was finished but the difficulties with the water level proved to be worse than anticipated. Cornelius Osterhout wrote, July 21, 1837: "Dear Sir: I tak the Liberty to wirte once more Respecting that mill After a Long and teadious wnter an Springs work I have finished your Contract and have spent all the money I was worth in this world and am still a goodeal in Deat. the whole job cost me about 7000 Dollars. Tharefore I hope you will Consider me alittle. Besides the Extreas that is now my Due I am verry much in want for I am way hear in the woods and

not a bent of money and not a foot of
Land and no pork. I can earn but verry
little with the mill on the acount of
Low water. Thar is not near anough for
one wheal in the Day time. Consequentley
you see I am in a purty Bad fix. Spent
all my money and all most my Life too
for to git you and myself too out of a
Bad Bargain with the Expectation of soon
Replacing it with the profits of the
mill wich I shall fail in verry much.
Pleas to write me as soon as you git
this . . . C. Osterhout"

The dateline on the letter is Whiting,
Allegan County. There is no record of a
Whiting in Allegan County, but postal
records show that there was a post
office in Van Buren County named
Whiting, from September 25, 1837, to
September 30, 1838, and that Cornelius
Osterhout was postmaster. There was also
an Osterhout Lake later in the southern
portion of Lee Township, Allegan County.
less than two miles from the Van Buren
County border. This would indicate that
the sawmill was probably located in
Geneva Township, Van Buren County,
somewhere along the middle branch of the
Black River.

Osterhout wrote again in November of
1838 starting his plea with, "I have had
hard struggling" and explaining that the
mill dam ran over and washed partly
away the previous fall, undermining the
structure of the mill building. He said
he had moved to government land and was
making shingles. The heartfelt pleas
must have moved John Allen, because
while he owed money to a great many
others that fall of 1838, he sent

Osterhout the $600 that was due him.

Other Lands

In addition to the parcels listed above John Allen also owned land in Columbia, Arlington, and Hamilton Townships of Van Buren County. As the money problem worsened most of these smaller tracts were simply abandoned and later sold for taxes. As recently as 1919 Van Buren County lawyers were searching for the heirs of John Allen to secure quit claim deeds to clear the titles.

Other Michigan Dreams

John Allen bought land with as much enthusiasm as a child might collect sea shells at the beach. Even during times when his creditors were clamoring for cash, he continued to purchase government land, lots and tracts from individuals, and occasionally an interest in the dreams of others.

Spring Arbor

John may have owned some land in the vicinity of Jacksonburgh, later Jacksonapolis, still later simply Jackson, in Jackson County as early as 1833. When the County of Jackson was getting organized in 1830, he served with Henry Rumsey and Chauncey S. Goodrich, on a commission to locate the seat of justice. They recommended that it be located in Jacksonapolis which had been designated the county seat four months earlier. He was also present on the first Tuesday in September, 1832, when the first session of the court was opened with pomp and oratory by Judge Oliver Ross in the parlor of early settler Horace Blackman. John Allen served as attorney in the first case presented, that of John Doe, a tavern keeper, who was charged with selling liquor to an Indian. The defendant was later found guilty and fined $20.

In August of 1836 John Allen purchased for $3000 a large tract in section 29 of Spring Arbor Township, Jackson County, from Samuel A. Sperry. Later additional land was purchased in sections 31 and 32. The project was a company effort and John's associates included Rev. Henry Colclazer, Luther W. Guiteau, Benjamin H. Packard (who was instrumental in the founding of Jackson), William Smith, Samuel A. Sperry, Sarah L. Taylor, William R. Thompson, and Aaron Vance. John Allen, with the assistance of his brother Turner, who sometimes did surveying, was authorized to lay out the lots. The investors agreed that profits from the venture would be distributed on the basis of one-twelfth for each investor, except for Allen who would receive two- twelfths in recognition of his work in surveying and acting as land agent. As noted in the 1836 deed, the land was held in his name.

The company land was about 400 acres and included land in the southwest quarter of section 29, the northwest quarter of section 32 directly to the south, and the eastern half of the northeast quarter of section 31 to the west of section 32. The land formed an inverted L with the village situated on what would later be called the Sears Road. The company decided to call their village Spring Arbour (later Arbor) the name of the township, so called because of numerous springs in the area. This site included an Indian burial ground which the new settlers carefully fenced and protected. The name Spring Arbor had first been applied to a townsite begun in 1835 in the top half of section 29 by Benjamin Packard and William Smith. Both Smith and Packard were investors in the new venture.

Benjamin Packard was born in Royalton, Vermont, July 10, 1788, and left home in 1808 with his brother Silas to "seek his fortune." After his arrival in the State of New York he studied to become a physician and was the first resident doctor in Royalton, New York. He came to Michigan in 1821 with his wife, the former Eleanor Royce, and their daughter Caroline Matilda and eventually settled in Ann Arbor until becoming one of the founding fathers of Jackson in 1829. His daughter married pioneer preacher Elijah H. Pilcher in 1835. Packard was one of three individuals who applied in 1835 for a charter to begin a Methodist Seminary in Spring Arbor, to be called the Spring Arbor Seminary. (The other two in the project were both Methodist clergymen: his son-in-law Elijah Pilcher and the Rev. Henry Colclazer, also investors in the new town). The charter was granted March 23, 1835, and early college records show that 173 acres were donated in Spring Arbor Township for its erection. Some accounts assert that at least a portion of a foundation was completed, but funds were slow in coming, and many potential donors did not like the Spring Arbor site. On April 12, 1835, the Michigan legislature passed an act amending the first charter, that changed the name to Wesleyan Seminary, and the location to Albion. Packard, Pilcher and Colclazer continued their support of the school, Packard served several years on the board of trustees and Colclazer was the first librarian. The program of the Wesleyan Seminary was later expanded and it became Albion College in 1861.

In planning Spring Arbor John used his experience at Ann Arbor as a model and apparently offered free building lots to mechanics and artisans. In February of 1837 John received a letter from Benjamin H. Packard, asking that deeds be issued to James Taylor, a tailor, and Sylvester Abbott, a merchant. The letter included a drawing showing the public square, and the location of the two shops.

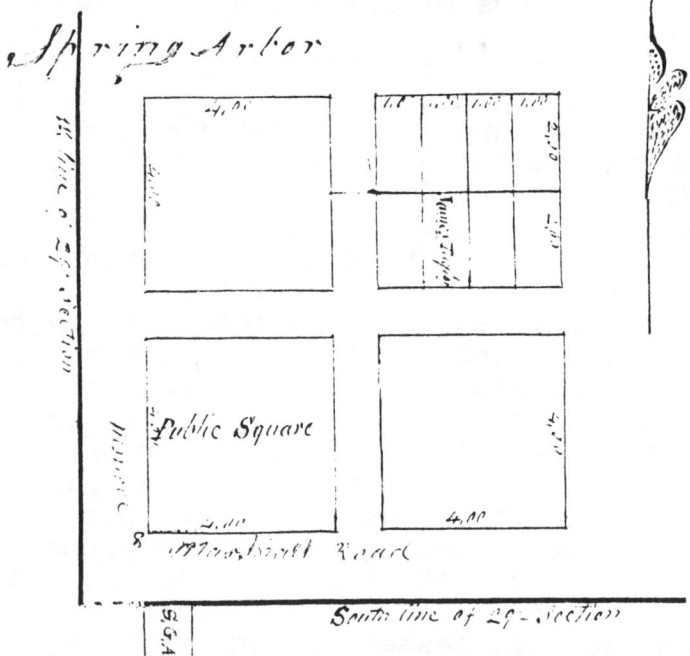

Packard's Map of downtown Spring Arbor marking the position of Taylor's tailor shop (upper right block).

James A. Taylor was an Englishman by birth, who had served the apprenticeship required to become a tailor in England. He and his wife Rachel came to America in 1835. Leaving his wife in Churchville, Monroe County, New York, Taylor came west looking for a new home. His journey brought him to Michigan and Spring Arbor. On June 4, 1835, he wrote:

Dear Wife Companion and Friend I received your letter May 30 and was glad to here from you. . . I thought to sart from here the 4 of June but work came in and others wished me to stay til after the independec the 4 of July to make sum thin clous for them so I stay til 6 of July in this place I have made choys of 2 Vilige lots the cost of the 2 will be 35 dollars in work this place was once none by the name of Indian Villeg the Indians had ther wigworms here made of bark sevrel of them but are now distride but ther is sum Indian Chefs graves on a hill five bodes I think wich the white men have so fenced round that pigs and boys can not distrod the bons and this pleses the red men well wen they came past the squas pated the ground . . . This place is now cald Spring Arber on account of the many springs round the vesinety I think this a butiful cuntry and with

respecting to temprenc and
morels thes place esccels all
for its sise. . . the Villig
is gust lad out in lots ther
is a black smith a Deter
(doctor) and a shumaker came
in wen I did and we work both
in one shop . . . ther no
frame bilders in the place at
present but ther is 2 frames
will be up sun the shumaker
got his frame part made ther
is a mill prievilige a mile
south of this a stream of
spring warter and it dose not
frese the spring warter ther
is land give or siuld for a
Mathedest Simenery. . . Dear
Wife get redey as much as you
can sel all the things you can
that we can not conventley
carety pact up for the cost of
teming is hie wen I com I
don't want to say no longer
than I can help for I have
promes a grat del of work in
the faul and I can not do much
now for ther is no trimings in
the place and it wold be well
for me to bing sum with me
ther is some talk of a stor
being sarted this sumer and a
temprance tavern. . .

The site was near the very beginning
of the Kalamazoo River, a major Michigan
stream. The river begins in Jackson
County and runs diagonally across the
northeast corner of section 31 as it
begins its trek across the southern part
of the state, eventually emptying into
Lake Michigan at Saugatuck 120 miles to

the west. Part of the plan called for a canal (or mill race) that would join Cross Lake (in section 32) with the north branch of the Kalamazoo River "where the land is best suited for mill purposes." In 1836 rights were obtained from Solomon Wolcott to cross his land with the canal "sufficient wide and deep."

It would appear that construction of the mill proceeded slowly. In December of 1836, B. H. Packard wrote angrily: "I am now suffering on account of money I have advanced, and still more (in feelings) on account of debts that the company owes where I am holder. One hundred dollars due to the old Bank of Michigan for our mill I ran, but not a dollar can I get to pay it. How shall I get pay for boarding men, drawing timber and lumber for the mill, advancing money, etc. Shall I sell the frame mill, gears, etc. to do these things or how? Something I shall do and that soon. . . Dear Sir: You will recollect that I have not had the first hundred dollars note and the second payment is due day after tomorrow." He finished the letter with, "No map, no nothing, and we know nothing what to do."

The map finally arrived in February of 1837, and even that was a disaster. William Smith, postmaster of Spring Arbor, wrote that the lithographed drawings contained "a number of essential errors" so as to make them worthless.

The mill was still unfinished in March of 1837 when John received a letter from William Maynard (later mayor of Ann Arbor), who had just purchased an interest in the Spring Arbor property, with news that "we are about making an effort to complete the mill &c and for that purpose have hired Sperry to move out and superintend the work." Indications are that it was still not completed in November of 1838, when John Allen and his wife Ann Isabella Allen (one of the few times her name appeared on a deed), conveyed to William S. Maynard, the "rights for constructing a mill race and damming the Kalamazoo River for mill purposes in Spring Arbor Township, property formerly owned by Benjamin H. Packard, William O. Cross, Solomon Wolcott, etc. . . "

The 1838 Blois Gazetteer of the State

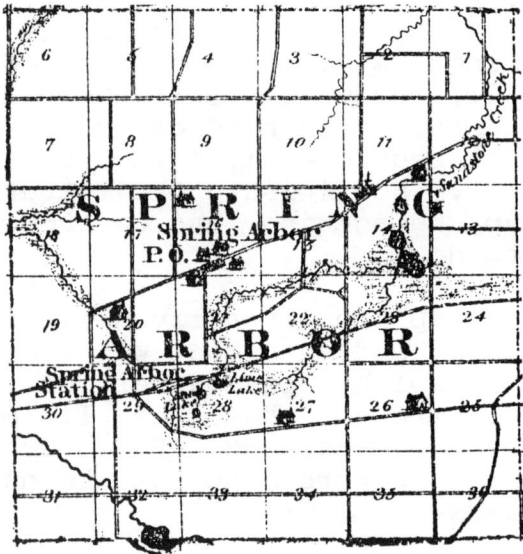

An 1881 map showing two Spring Arbors.

of Michigan describes "Spring Arbour" as "Village and post office, in a township of the same name, county of Jackson, situated near one of the head branches of the Kalamazoo river, at the site of an ancient Indian village, and in the midst of burr oak plains. Here is a store, 2 physicians, and a few families."

(Spring Arbor, which never did become an incorporated village, continued to meander around the township. An 1840 map shows the settlement at the first site on the north edge of section 29, an 1858 map puts it up on the territorial road in section 16, an 1874 map marks both places, and an 1881 map puts Spring Arbor P.O. in section 16 and Spring Arbor Station, on the Michigan Central Air Line, in section 29. The settlement left in 1988 is located in section 16 on the state highway and includes Spring Arbor College.)

Grand Haven

According to Franklin Everett in his Memorials of the Grand River Valley: "There was a rush of settlers into the Grand River Valley in 1836 and thereabouts, and a furor for locating lands as a speculative investment." John Allen and his friend, Henry Morgan of Aurora, Cayuga County, New York were determined to be part of that furor.

Some time prior to January of 1836 they had apparently made a deal with Louis Campau, the founder of Grand Rapids who also held a lot of land on

the south bank near the mouth of Grand
River at a small settlement called Grand
Haven in Ottawa County. It would appear
that the terms of the contract demanded
that Allen and Morgan build a house on
their land by July 1, 1836. A letter
from Morgan to Allen, dated January 7,
1836, proposes: "In relation to the
House which we are to build by the 1st

*Campau's Addition to Grand Haven, the
lots in Allen's contract are numbered 1
through 5 in center on the riverfront.*

July next I have to say, it is thought
best for you to write Mr. Farry or some
other person of your acquaintance at

Grand Haven to have the work commenced and finished with all possible expedition. We ought not to go over $500 outlay in building such a house as is contemplated. In looking at my papers I do not find any paper prescribing the size &c, &c, of the house and conclude you must have it among yours. Nor do I recollect that it is stated what kind, size, &c, of a house particularly we are to build and therefore am more particular in calling your mind to the subject of expending not more than the 500 and of using as much less as possible in building a decent small House. . . Would it not be wise for you to write to Mr. Campau and get the time for building the House extended in case it should so happen that we cannot get it done by 1st July -- but if he would not so extend time -- then let us "go ahead" and complete it in time to save all troubles." (Mr. Farry was Rev. William Ferry, the first settler in Grand Haven who had arrived in 1834.)

The house is not mentioned in a contract dated March 5, 1836, in which Campau agreed to sell to Allen and Morgan five lots in the Village of Grand Haven near the mouth of the Grand River, extending to the middle of the channel, for $10,000 with the provision that at least $1,000 be paid to him by September 1. Campau, who was known as a shrewd businessman, even made a provision that the money could be paid to a bank in New York "provided it is paid anytime between this and the first day of August next." An alternative repository for payment was the Bank at Bronson, one of Michigan's fabled wildcat banks.

There is another contract in the Allen papers that conveys to John Allen additional lots near the mouth of the Grand River, and what was popularly called the "lower diggings," and also "the privilege of wharfing the end of Howard Street into the channel of Grand River for public use."

Despite the contracts, there are no receipts among the Allen papers, and the assumption is that the Grand Haven project was another that was lost in the economic Panic of 1837. The main part of the City of Grand Haven was upstream and by 1907 an atlas carried the comment, "There is little left of the lower diggings."

Ingham County

Having acquired the Washtenaw County seat for Ann Arbor, Allen was certainly aware of the value of that distinction to a town. In an April 1836 letter from Henry Morgan, one of his most eager investor friends in New York, he was asked: "As to our Michigan enterprises, let me inquire who has got the county seat of Ingham County? And how near to it is our location? And whether the county seat of Ottawa has been located? And where? The same as to Van Buren Co? . . Should you be successful in your County Seat, let me in, as we talked."

The county seat of Ingham county was located in the winter of 1835-6 at a settlement called Ingham, in Vevay Township. It was owned by Charles Thayer

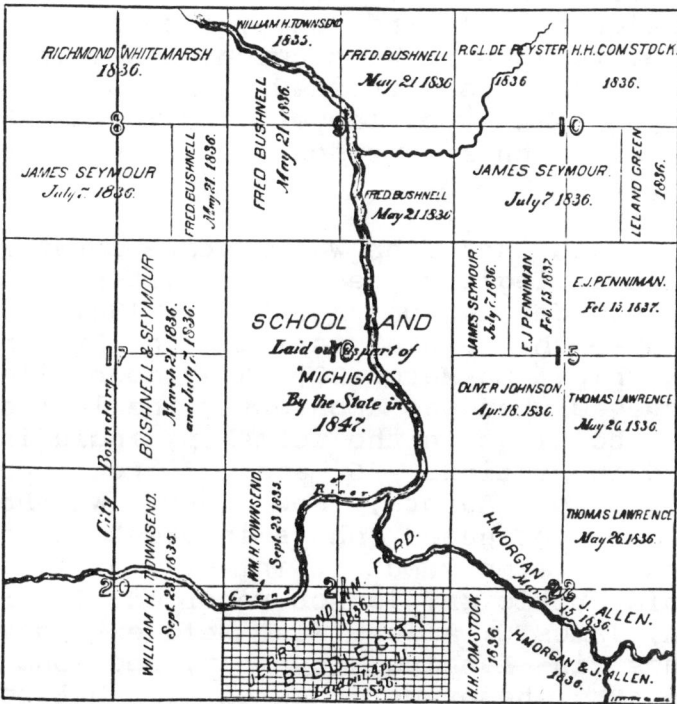

Map labels (reading by section):

RICHMOND WHITEMARSH 1836.

WILLIAM H. TOWNSEND 1833.

FRED. BUSHNELL May 21 1836.

R.G.L. DE PEYSTER 1836

H.H. COMSTOCK 1836.

JAMES SEYMOUR July 7 1836.

FRED BUSHNELL May 21 1836.

FRED BUSHNELL May 21 1836.

JAMES SEYMOUR July 7 1836.

FRED BUSHNELL May 21 1836.

LELAND GREEN 1836.

BUSHNELL & SEYMOUR March 2 1836. and July 1836.

SCHOOL LAND Laid out as part of 'MICHIGAN By the State in 1847.

JAMES SEYMOUR July 7 1836.

E.J. PENNIMAN Feb 13 1837.

E.J. PENNIMAN Feb 13 1837.

OLIVER JOHNSON Apr. 18 1836.

THOMAS LAWRENCE May 26 1836.

City Boundary.

WILLIAM H. TOWNSEND Sept 23 1835.

JNO H. TOWNSEND Sept 23 1833.

River

Grand

THOMAS LAWRENCE May 26 1836.

H MORGAN March 15 1836.

J. ALLEN 1836.

JERRY AND H. 1836

BIDDLE CITY

H.H. COMSTOCK 1836.

H MORGAN & J. ALLEN 1836.

A map from the Durant history showing original purchasers of the land where Lansing was later built.

and it never developed beyond a cross-roads. In 1840 the county seat was moved to the Village of Mason. Allen and Morgan, however, narrowly missed an even bigger prize. On March 15, 1836, the pair purchased slightly over half of section 22 in Lansing Township, where Sycamore Creek joins the Red Cedar River just upstream from its confluence with the Grand River. In 1847 the capitol of the State of Michigan was located just

97

to the northwest. Their entire former
claim is now part of downtown Lansing.
The tract in section 22 may have been a
portion of the land conveyed on July 15,
1836, to John P. Huntington of New York.
The deed was witnessed by James Kingsley, an Ann Arbor lawyer, and Thomas W.
McCue, John's stepson on a visit from
Virginia.

In 1847 John was a state senator,
and the legislature voted after pro-
longed debate on March 9, 1847, to
locate the state capital in Lansing
Township. On March 22, 1847, John Allen
conveyed what was apparently the last of
his holdings in the township, including
land in sections 26 and 27 to Henry
Morgan of Aurora, New York. Whether
Morgan purchased John's interest in the
land, or simply put it in his name to
avoid criticism, is not recorded. John's
son, James C. Allen, also held extensive
lands in Lansing Township, sections 1
and 2. These were purchased between
March 12, 1847 and October 28, 1848,
after the location of the capital was
known.

One of the properties that was
listed in a tentative sales agreement
with two Oswego men in June of 1837 was
"about six hundred acres of land on the
Red Cedar River where the State road
crosses said River at Ten dollars an
acre." One of the two, R. L. Lawrence,
purchased 150 acres and wrote John Allen
in August of 1837: "I got 150 acres on
the Red Cedar River, my proposal. . .
let me have the remaining 150 acres of
that parcel and take in exchange for it
the two shares I have in the village of

98

Mason, you making up the difference of $500 in lots in South Haven."

Henry Morgan and John Allen, about 1836, purchased government land in sections 25, 26, 35, and 36, on the eastern edge of Meridian Township, where the Red Cedar River crosses the road from Detroit. This later included the village of Meridian, where the first post office in the township was established in 1841. John sold his share of the Meridian Township lands to Joseph Hunt of Oswego, New York, in 1837. In 1848 Henry Morgan sold most of his interest in the land to Richard, Edwin, and George P. Morgan, all of Aurora, New York, apparently relatives.

Eaton County

Early land records show that John Allen owned several large parcels of land in Eaton County purchased in 1836 and 1837. His holdings were located in Hamlin and Eaton Rapids Townships.

He was indirectly responsible for the settling of Benton Township. Japhet Fisher, the first settler in that township, had come to Michigan directly from the City of New York to work in the clearing of Richmond, one of Allen's Allegan County projects. He earned $266 which he used to purchase land, according to a county history, "besides paying $49.75 to one of the settlers in Charlotte for a barrel of flour and a half barrel of pork." The history also relates that he was fond of going barefoot and other settlers would test the toughness of his feet at barn

99

raisings or other social occasions, with the largest bull thistles they could find. Edward A. Foote reminisced in 1876: "Japhet with his full rosy cheeks, laughing and talking and lifting, would seem perfectly unconscious of the fact that his bare foot was crushing the fangs of one of those savage thistles, and that all were looking at him either to wince, or look down, or move his foot to some more comfortable place."

Calhoun County

John Allen was also a landholder in Calhoun county, in the same tier of counties as Washtenaw, just to the west of Jackson County.

The record of early land transactions in Calhoun County shows that Cephas Smith, Isaac N. Hurd, and John Allen, all of Washtenaw County, purchased 80 acres in Marshall Township, Calhoun County, from Jonathan Wood of Kalamazoo County, on February 22, 1831. On November 3, 1834, John Allen of Ann Arbor bought 80 acres from Henry W. Kellogg of Ann Arbor in section 13, Marshall Township.

Washtenaw County

In addition to his extensive landholdings in Ann Arbor Township, John Allen owned large tracts of land in Pitt Township, just south of the settlement of Ann Arbor (later Pittsfield Township). Early land records show that on March 28, 1825, he purchased 104.08 acres of land in section 4, and 320 acres in section 9. In May of 1825 he bought 160 acres in section 17, and an additional 80 acres in section 4.

Later, June 33, 1833, he became the owner of 80 acres in Freedom Township southwest of Ann Arbor Township. This may have been what his son, James C., later referred to as "the farm."

Kalamazoo County

In the Calhoun County land records it is recorded that Cephas A. Smith, Isaac N. Hurd and John Allen purchased 80 acres of land in Kalamazoo County near what would later be the settlement of Bronson, on February 5, 1831. But John had a more important role in Kalamazoo County than land speculator. Late in 1830 he and Calvin Smith were appointed by terri- torial governor Lewis Cass to locate the county seat for Kalamazoo Coun- ty. In a report written January 15, 1831, at Ann Arbor they recommended a spot "on an eminence near the center of the southwest quarter of section 15. . . owned by Titus Bronson, Esquire," on the condition that Bronson set apart land

Titus Bronson

for a courthouse, jail, academy, common schools, burial ground, and four squares of eight rods each for the first four

that region. He refused to sell any of his potatoes there, retaining them for seed, but he paid his board in potatoes, and his hostess carved the eyes out and planted them, before adding the rest to the stew pot. For several years he roamed through Ohio and Michigan as a sort of "Johnny Appleseed" of the potato, but in 1829 he decided to settle in Kalamazoo County and became the founder of Kalamazoo. He originally named the town Bronson, after himself, but in 1836 those who opposed his manners and policies had the name changed to Kalamazoo, taking the title of the river and county.

(There were a number of other Allens active in early Michigan, and at least three others were named John. A John Allen was the earliest settler in Huron County building a mill, with Alanson Daggett, in the spring of 1837 at a place called Rock Falls, near the present-day town of Harbor Beach. A John Allen also settled in Lenawee County at an early date, and another was an early land purchaser in Ingham and Eaton counties. These families were apparently not related to the Allens of Virginia.)

*

Interlude in New York

During the 1830s land speculation was widespread on the frontier. Sales of public lands increased dramatically. In the record year of 1835, the total (for the whole country) was nearly triple of any previous year. Proceeds of 1836 were equal to the total of 1820 to 1833 combined. Most of the purchases were speculative in nature. As the price of land rose, the true settler lost interest, and the land speculator began to back off too. Many of John Allen's clients were eastern investors and he felt that if he could get in closer contact with them, the large portfolio of lands that he had for sale could be marketed in a more businesslike fashion.

Elizabeth Tate Allen, John's mother, wrote in September of 1836 to her grandson James C. Allen, then attending school in New York State: "Your pa is in a grate notion of going to New York and taking you all with him. I don't like it much. I don't know what he is going to do with me. . . He has made up his mind to go and take your ma and the girls. I'm not sure I will let Elizabeth go." (Elizabeth, John's daughter by his first marriage, had always lived with her grandparents.)

It was a difficult time to leave. After a brief skirmish with the State of Ohio about the southern boundary Michigan was still struggling with the paperwork involved in becoming a state. An act to admit Michigan to the Union, calling for certain boundary compromises, was passed by Congress, June 15, 1836. The Congressional document was rejected at a Territorial meeting held in Ann Arbor on September 15. A second ratification meeting (unauthorized and probably illegal) was called for December 14, also at Ann Arbor. This time the compromise passed and Michigan was admitted to the Union, although it had already been functioning as a state for nearly two years. There was, for a time, much speculation that Ann Arbor would be chosen as the capitol of the new state. A map of the village drawn in 1836 designates a State House Square at the corner of William and State Streets, but a decision locating a state capitol was delayed by the new legislature until 1847.

In the midst of this political activity John Allen's financial problems were coming to a head. The November 7, 1836, *Ann Arbor Argus* carried notice of a sheriff's sale of certain property of John Allen to satisfy debts. The list of items to be sold included: "one pair dunn horses, harness and double wagon with wrought iron axletrees, one pair of chestnut horses with their harness and double wagon with cast iron axletrees, one span white horses, and one pair of bay carriage horses and light stage wagon; one span light brown horses with

104

their harness, one pair brown mares with harness, also a light lumber wagon, iron axletrees." The sale was set for December 5, 1836. That the sale was necessary was a symbol of John's declining financial fortunes, but the long list of livestock and items available speaks to the success of the Ann Arbor project.

In a letter dated November 19, 1836, Ann Allen wrote her son who had just returned to Virginia after a visit: "Mr. Allen returned the middle of the week you left. He has purchased a small carriage for us to go to New York in. James the Hostler goes in a Lumber Waggon and carries our baggage. I try again to get Rachel to go but her Father wont consent. [Rachel was apparently a serving girl Ann had asked to accompany them, but Rachel's father would not give her permission to go.] We start next Monday to go by land, to New York go from here to Monroe, then intersect the national road some where in Ohio. There was quite a fall of snow here yesterday, a dull prospect for good roads (I dread my journey) but I think it is for the best to go by land, it has got so late to cross the Lake."

In contrast to her mother and grandmother, 14-year-old Sarah Ann seemed to think that the move to the big city was a fine idea. Following their arrival she wrote to her stepbrother, Thomas McCue: "We have arrived here safe. And I am much pleased with the City; what little I have seen of it. We had quite a pleasant trip. I will give you a short description of it. We came

in our own carriage to Columbia in
Pennsylvania. We had also a lumber
waggon to carry our baggage in. James
drove the cream colour horses in the
baggage waggon. And Pa drove the white
horses, in the carriage to Columbia,
then we took the railroad to
Philadelphia and took our baggage with
us, and James went with the carriage and
four horses round on the turnpike, then
we took the steam boat to Borden town,
from there we went in a car to Amboy,
from there in a steam boat to New York.
I like riding in the Car very much; but
the steam boat I can say I do not like
as well. . . Pa bought a house and we
are in it cleaning and every thing is in
a bustle." (It would appear that John
was able to rescue some of the carriage
horses from the December sale.)

At the end of Sarah's letter her
mother penned a note describing the
journey as "pleasant for the time of
year" but "fatiguing for me." She
describes the house as "pleasant
convenient quite up in the city" and

Ann Allen's fan.

tells Thomas that she hopes that Mrs. Mahand who had once stayed with the Allens in Ann Arbor remembers her. "It would be of advantage to me, as she moves in such society as I have always been accustomed to." She gives the address of the house as 39 North 14th Street, near 7th Avenue (it would now probably be West 14th Street).

For his real estate business John rented an office at 44 Wall Street. Because his company was later called the American Exchange Co., and his office was located just two doors down from the first permanent home of the New York Stock and Exchange Board at 40 Wall Street, some Michigan historians have credited him with being one of the founding fathers of the New York Stock Exchange. Although John was willing to make a dollar on anything saleable, his dealings were mainly in real estate. The New York Stock Exchange was founded in 1817. He had a few clients at his new office. In June of 1837 John wrote a lengthy presale contract with two Oswego, New York, men offering them shares in the Richmond Company (an Allegan county venture), lots in the Village of Mason (in Van Buren County), land on the Red Cedar River (Ingham County), and/or village lots in South Haven (Van Buren County). It is doubtful if any other broker in New York City had as varied a menu of Michigan lands.

In March of 1837 John purchased a "three story brick dwelling house" on Broadway a little farther uptown.

By mid-summer the economic rumblings had turned into what came to be known as the Panic of 1837. The main factors of the panic, economists stated later with the benefits of hindsight, were the debts caused by a flood of railroad and canal building, the closure of the Bank of the United States which had brought some stability to the currency, and the Specie Circular, an edict from President Andrew Jackson decreeing that after July 11, 1836, nothing but gold or silver would be accepted in payment for government land. It was the land speculator who was hardest hit.

Franklin Everett later described the times in *Memorials of the Grand River Valley*: "Lots were held and sold at fabulous prices. . . Speculators were greedily buying up land and lots. No matter if a man did owe a few thousand dollars; he had the land and the lots, which were sure to double their value in a year. . . It was a splendid bubble -- it was an enormous bubble. The banks, in the shape of expanded loans had furnished the gas, and ten million pairs of lungs were strained for its inflation. All at once the bubble burst, and the banks, speculators, merchants, all found themselves gaping and gazing into blank space. . . It was all black; there is no use coloring it. Land and lots would not sell for anything. Debts alone were undiminished. As a consequence, about all failed. So general was this the rule, that the man who had not failed was almost ashamed to walk the streets, so woefully was he out of fashion."

John Allen was not "out of fashion."
In May of 1837 he mortgaged his
furniture for $1,000 with the provision
that he would be allowed "peaceable
possession" for one year. He had
apparently written his son in Ann Arbor
that they would return to Michigan in
the spring. In a letter dated February
24, 1837, James C. asks what time in the
spring, and adds: "Father, I have
concluded to go on the farm in the
spring if you are willing. I do not
think my health will permit of me being
any thing else but a farmer -- I have
studied this winter all that my health
would permit, Elizabeth is quite unwell,
she has a cough and there is some
appearance of her disease returning, she
looks quite bad. . . I would like to
know whether you expect to take
Elizabeth to New York when you return
there, I suppose Grandmother will go to
Uncle Turners if you do, for she says
she does not want to go to the farm with
me." James then devotes a page to the
problems of living at his grandmother's
with Aunt Polly's children,"She will
neither make them mind, nor let any one
else," and ends the letter, "Father, do
write soon and tell me all the news and
give me some advice on the subjects I
have mentioned or on any other you think
proper."

Instead of advice he received a letter
from his father dated August 14, 1837,
that was apparently delivered by a Mr.
Cormerais of Boston. John wrote that it
was still possible that he would arrive
in Ann Arbor on August 28 as planned but
"my business here is now in such a shape
that it would be death to my future

prospects to leave at this time -- We have just started a Co. called "The American Exchange Company" which belongs mostly to me and now while it is just getting underway, I dare not leave it."

In frantic penstrokes John urges his son to make Mr. Cormerais comfortable, and to help him and Mr. Maynard raise $1,500 to pay the "Sutton claims" which had to be paid by the 28th. "If Mr. M will raise the money to pay it and wants it immediately -- you must put your Shoulder to the wheel and put every note, Judgment, Horse, Cows, family utensils, Hay, grain, in short every thing you have there -- if necessary not excepting Elizabeth's piano -- to pay the debt. If it is not paid the sacrifice is the whole of the land by the Village. And then I wish you to Settle up your affairs there and as early as possible before it becomes dangerous -- come with your Sister to the City -- without waiting for me. . . This is my desire James and let the Sacrifice be what it may -- regard it not, I will make it up. For as to raising money here at present it is out of the question. I explained to Mr. Maynard the reasons more in detail why I still to the last moment leaned on my own resources here for the payment of that debt. . . If worst comes to the worst and nothing else can be done, I have given Mr. C my note at 4 months for two thousand dollars which he must sell to raise the money which note I have made payable to your order and you will have to sign. I hope, however, that Mr. M. will raise the money for a few days until you and he can sell stuff enough

110

to replace it -- which would be the better course."

There is no mention of the farm, but in a postscript he adds, "When you come down with your Sister, if you do not like the City you may return to Michigan." He also notes that Ann and Sarah Ann are in Lexington, Virginia, visiting John and Thomas McCue, " as to the time of their return, nothing is yet fixed upon determinedly." In a second letter dated August 17 to James, his father recommends that Elizabeth return to New York with Mr. Comerais, and tells them that he had traded for a small place in the country one and a half miles from the city, "If when you come you would prefer to stay there you can have your choice." And adds a note, "Tell Elizabeth not to worry about her piano as I have one here for her worth double that one."

William Woodbridge

In a letter to William Woodbridge of Detroit, who was attorney for John in the Harford case, but also represented others to whom John owed money, he wrote in September of 1837, that he would have answered his letter sooner "only for the confusion in which it found us, in removing from one part of the city to another--I have, ever since my arrival in this great metropolis, lived in almost daily expectation of visiting Michigan -- but the pecuniary embarrassments of the country -- the scarcity of money &c -- have up to the present time found me unprepared."

He was willing to try anything. January 11, 1838, John wrote Lucius Lyon, then U. S. Senator from Michigan, for assistance in procuring the proper applications for a patent. He told Lyon he had been promised an interest in a new fuel compound, that would burn more thoroughly than common wood, if he would assist the inventor in obtaining a patent.

James C. seems to have begged off the trip to New York, but Elizabeth had arrived by January of 1838, and was as enthralled with the city as her younger sister had been. She wrote James: "My health is good and I feel quite contented. I often think of home and would like much to be with you, but I hope it may be for my improvement to be in the city." She and her father had rented their house to a family in exchange for their board and that of the Broom family who also resided there. They had rented it to a Quaker family, but "they do not set a good table, and in many other respects do not suit us -- we are trying to get some one else." There were three Broom daughters and they were special friends to Elizabeth. "We promenade on Broadway often, sometimes to do a little shopping or to make calls. In fact we often have no business but to see the fashions, and inhale the refreshing breezes."

She concludes her letter to James, "Pa has given me several handsome books which he took for a debt and a beautiful album -- Pa is well, he has but little business to attend to. I hope he will give you the farm."

James C. had another advocate in his quest for the life of a farmer. His uncle, James Turner Allen, wrote John in February of 1838, apologizing that he had to use two notes he held against John to pay some debts of his own, and asking that John pay them when they are presented "if it is among the possibilities." And he adds, "James C. thinks you come out rather hard upon him in the letter you wrote to me and directed to him, and I think myself you do not act wisely with regard to him. I cannot see for the life of me what you want him to go to New York for. It is the last place I would want a son of mine to go, especially when he is so much opposed to it himself -- he is now of age and wants to be doing for himself and it is not unnatural that it should be so. And if it was my case I would be glad to encourage him by aiding him all that I could and I think if you would reflect on the subject you will come to the same conclusion."

James C. remained in Michigan, and eventually moved to a farm near Tecumseh. John continued to depend on the young man, as a Michigan agent, and in a July 16, 1838, letter to Detroit's William Woodbridge assures the judge that James "will attend to the requested payment immediately," then adds, "As in money matters -- to use a common saying -- "I am used up" -- You are so far removed at Detroit from the great center of monied operations, that you do not feel the effects of the great flood, tides and ebbs. . . I have at length determined on returning to Michigan -- and try the bush once more -- It is the safe place, through such times as those we have passed through."

John had another reason that made his return to Michigan a sound business idea. In 1836 he had fallen in with three Eastern capitalists who owned a lot of pine lands in Allegan County and who had dreams of building a milling center on the Kalamazoo River that would rival any yet constructed in western Michigan. They needed a representative to go to the area, superintend the work, and sell the land. And they were convinced that John Allen was their man.

Richmond

In late 1835 or early 1836 Lucius Boltwood and Luke Sweetser of Amherst, Massachusetts, Henry Morgan of Aurora, New York, Charles Moseley of Ann Arbor, and John Allen formed the Richmond Company (apparently named in honor of the capital of Virginia) and purchased 2,240 acres in Allegan County on the north side of the Kalamazoo River just west of its confluence with the Rabbit River and about seven miles from its mouth on Lake Michigan. On this site they platted an elaborate town and bragged in their printed material: "This place has advantages not possessed by any Town, Village or City in the State combining the navigation of the Lakes by Steam boats of the first class with water power sufficient to drive one hundred saws. . . " There were five mills spaced across the termination of a mile-long mill race, 66 foot streets, and hundreds of village building lots.

In May of 1836, for unknown reasons, Moseley withdrew from the project, and the remaining investors agreed to pay him the sum of $20,000 "at the time when a Saw Mill is put into opperation." Until the mill was operational, the contract specified that Moseley would continue to participate in the costs.

In the summer of 1836 expectations were running high and Luke Sweetser wrote: "I am glad to hear you have made a survey and find the water power beyond our expectations. . .What estimate do you propose to put upon lots? What improvement do you intend making this season? From what we learn from Michigan the country is filling up with actual settlers very fast -- are you making any roads to Richmond so that they may find their way there?"

The land was surveyed and platted and an order for maps of Richmond given to C. B. Graham of New York City for 600 impressions on paper and four on imperial silk. The map was designed to lure prospective investors and settlers. It shows 13 east-west streets including Pearl, Boltwood, Sweetser, Broken, Mechanics, High, Mill, State, Pine and Walnut. Running north and south the streets are numbered, First through 23rd. Five mills are depicted across the end of the mill race, and a short canal dredged to provide docking facilities for industry. In addition to the five men who formed the company Edwin Morgan is listed as one of the proprietors.

Printing in the right hand corner included the information that "Flour, Lumber or any other Manufactured article may be shipped from the mills to any port on the Lakes. There are extensive pineries on the Rabbit and Kalamazoo Rivers that are out of the reach of any other water power. Farming lands of the

116

first quality north and south of Richmond may be had at the government price, or a small advance." Another block of copy promised, "The Episcopalians, Methodist, Baptist and Presbyterian denominations are each entitled to two lots to be selected by the proprietors and deed on application of the Trustees of the respective Societies as soon as they are organized."

In July Boltwood wrote asking for a map of "our village" and urging Allen to faster action. Under the incorporation agreement John had been offered a tenth of the company; Boltwood offered him two-tenths, or one half of the whole property "if you operate to advantage."

In November of 1836 John Allen wrote a contract with Edwin R. Way and Ralph R. Mann "of Marshall and Richmond" to build a saw mill at Richmond and "put it into operation before September next." For this they were to receive the sum of $3,050. The contract was dated November 8, 1836, at Ann Arbor, and signed by Allen as agent for the company. J. F. Stratton was one of the witnesses. In the Allen files is a second paper with the same date which says tersely: "This certifies that the contract entered into between myself and John Allen dated at Ann Arbour for one years service -- is this day by Mutual consent cancelled. Ralph R. Mann."

Another contract was written on November 15, 1836, with J. F. Stratton, who had witnessed the Mann document, for "excavation of a mill race to carry the water from the Rabbit River at the foot of a bluff bank on the west side of the river on section 10, thence along the foot of said bluff bank." Stratton was also given a contract permitting him "to erect and build at his own proper cost and expense at Richmond a large two story public House for the accommodation of travellors." He was to be permitted to use lumber from the company mill, stone from their quarry, and given a building lot on which to construct the house "for the encouragement and accommodation of emigrants and visitors."

But it was Ralph Mann who was the first settler in the new village. According to an 1878 *Allegan Journal* article: "In 1836 Ralph R. Mann came down the Kalamazoo river in a flat boat from Marshall, in company with some others, bringing some groceries and dry goods, and provisions. . . Mr. Mann and his crew had an adventurous time coming down the river, clearing the river of trees lying across and doing his own piloting on the crooked stream with a Dutch crew that didn't understand English. He found an old French trading hut on the bank of the river, where there had been a trading post fifteen years before, at the end of his voyage, which he took for a residence for awhile." An 1880 Allegan County history added the information that "Twice during the trip from Kalamazoo to Richmond the craft ran upon rocks and came very near sinking, but the desperate exertions of the amateur mariners prevented this misfortune, and after a three weeks' journey the party landed safe and sound at Richmond." According to the county history John Allen and a party of people, including Ralph Mann's wife, who had traveled around by land, were there to meet them.

In a contract dated March 31, 1836, George Mayo of Bronson was engaged "to build for J. Allen a house to be made of logs 24 feet by 18 1 and 1/2 stories high covered with shakes. I am to cut out 1 door & 2 windows & lay one floor when the said Allen furnishes the lumber. I am to chink the same with mud & timber. The house is to be built at Rhodesville for which I am to receive $50." This house was apparently never completed because Allen never furnished the lumber. (Rhodesville must have been a name the Richmond Company considered in the naming of the village. On the outside of the above contract, in Allen's handwriting it was labeled, "Agreement to build house at Richmond.")

An agreement for the building of the first saw mill was signed December 5, 1836, with a provision to have it completed by "February next," including the clearing of one acre of grounds. It was at about this point in the development of the project that John Allen and family moved to New York City. What followed was two years of fervent correspondence between Allen, the investors, and on-the-site workers.

In December Moseley wrote: "Mr. Stratton has gone on with family and 8 or 10 men to commence opperations at Richmond. Not hearing from you after I had gotten the goods open & ready to sell I contracted with Austin & Barker

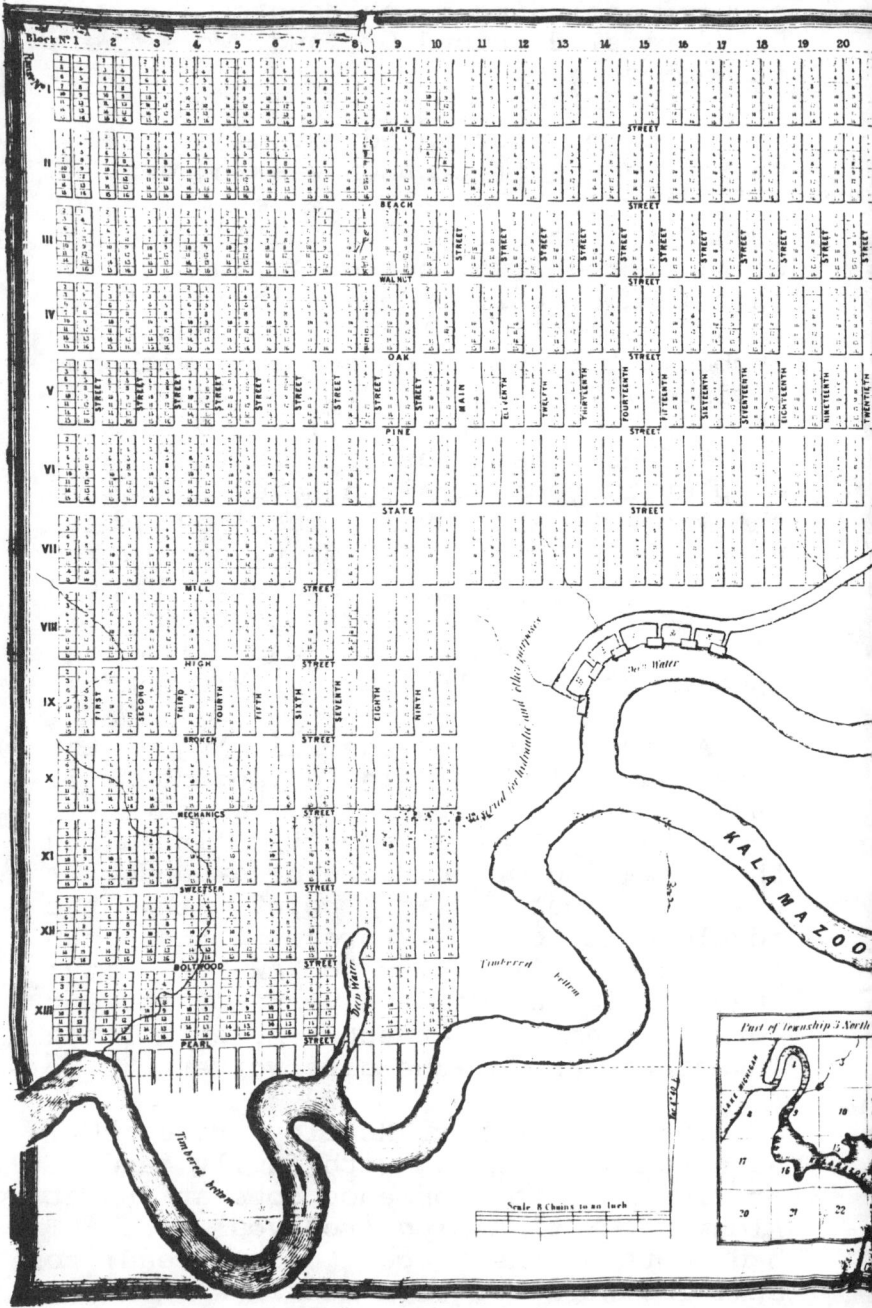

RICHMOND is situated on the Kalamazoo River, below its junction with the Rabbit River, five miles from Lake Michigan in the County of Allegan, State of Michigan.

This place has advantages not possessed by any Town, Village, or City in the State, combining, the navigation of the Lakes, by Steam boats of the first class, with water power sufficient to drive one hundred saws. Flour, Lumber, or any other Manufactured article, may be shipped from the mills to any part on the Lakes. There are extensive pineries on the Rabbit and Kalamazoo Rivers, that are out of the reach of any other water power. Farming lands of the first quality north and south of Richmond may be had at the government price, or a small advance

MILL RACE

RABBIT RIVER

RIVER

PLAN
of the Village of
RICHMOND
Allegan County
STATE of MICHIGAN

PROPRIETORS

Lucius Boltwood	Edwin Morgan
Luke Sweetser	John Allen
Henry Morgan	Charles Moseley

Part of Township 3 North Range 15 West

Note. All the Streets are 66 feet wide, except Sime and Water Streets which are 100 feet. Alleys 24 feet wide. The lots are all 66 by 120 feet except ...

to erect the frame of the proposed small sawmill calculating to have the mill & dam compleated in all the month of January. . . I gave Joseph & Timothy Barker a jobb of clearing off 10 acres along the bank to the river -- I perceive you directed James to procure the Mill Irons at Ypsilanti. I have mentioned to him two or three times that I wanted to see them started for the west before I go. He has finally observed that he had got no money & that he would not become responsible for them on a Credit. . . if James does not procure the Irons I shall take the liberty of getting them if I can borrow the money."

James was James C. Allen, John's son who remained behind in Ann Arbor. In a letter dated February 24, 1837, James assures his father, "Mr. Ball has been in and got the mill iron for the little mill at Richmond. Major Moseley says they are doing business there, they have got out all the timber for the mill and Ball has gone down there to draw it."

As the financial pinch of 1837 tightened the investors tried to continue, but times were hard. On January 17, 1837, Boltwood sent $250 to help cover expenses but wrote, "I hope you may be able to refund the money I now send before many months, as cash in this region is exceedingly scarce. I also hope you will dispose of our pine lands on such terms as will give us all a little of the needful."

In addition to the village site, near the confluence of the Rabbit and

Kalamazoo Rivers, the investors, as a group, singly and in pairs, owned hundreds of acres of pine lands in Allegan County. Tax records for 1836 and 1837 show Sweetser owned a large portion of Clyde Township, immediately to the south of Manlius Township where Richmond was located. John Allen owned 98 acres in Ganges Township, and 499 Acres in Saugatuck Township. Henry Morgan had purchased two quarter sections in Saugatuck Township, and, in partnership with Allen, owned additional parcels located in sections 23, 24, and 25. This second tract included 1,920 acres and touched the Kalamazoo River near what was later Mack's Landing. Allen also owned nearly a hundred acres in section 8 at the mouth of the Kalamazoo River on the south bank, across from a lighthouse near where Saugatuck's first settler, William G. Butler, ran a warehouse and transfer point. Because of constant shoaling the Kalamazoo River was only navigable by shallow draft boats most of the time, and cargo from lake steamers was usually lightered ashore and transferred to river boats. The Morgan Co. had 240 acres in Ganges Township and large tracts in Casco.

About the same time the Richmond project was getting under way, another rival company was preparing to build a mill near the mouth of the Kalamazoo River at a village they platted and called Singapore. The Singapore settlement included a wildcat bank, one of many that sprang up all over Michigan after the legislature eased the banking laws to require, instead of a full backing of gold, that the bank have on

123

deposit, sufficient specie to cover 30 percent of the bank notes issued. As Oshea Wilder, who worked for the Singapore investors, explained it to his bosses in New York: "Supposing from 20 to $50,000 of the bills were made payable at some office in New York, when issued here, if judiciously done, it would take an average of four months before they would reach New York for redemption when funds should be in readiness. . . "

In March of 1837 Moseley wrote to John in New York: "I have just returned from Richmond. Stratton appears to be doing well. All the laborers are employed by Stratton except the workers whom I have given a job of clearing ten acres along the Kalamazoo River. They have it nearly chopped for logging. I employed Austin by the Jobb to build the frame of the sawmill before I received information that Stratton had charge of the same. He however appeared satisfied with what I had done. They will probably have the mill running in four weeks. Austin's family are with him he is now building a frame house for himself near the store. After it is finished I have agreed to employ him by the day till October so you see there is no person now imployed by me only by Jobb consequently there has been no necessity of my being at Richmond during the winter. I agreed with Austin and R. R. Mann that each might erect a small frame house near the store that would be of use to the Company when they shall have selected their Lots That the Company should erect buildings of equal value in exchange for them. Mann has his timber drawn for his house and wishes to build a small Barn on the same principle. Stratton has already got out considerable timber & Logs for boards for his Large Tavern house. George Huntington appears healthy & contented . . . The fourth family have erected a log house about 60 Rods down the river from the store. The man is engaged in shoe making. R. R. Mann is appointed justice of the peace and will be a nuisance to our village. He calculates to keep tavern, sell whiskey and do any thing that a Lazy unprincipled man can devise to make a sixpence. He has boasted of his Right to dispossess Stratton on the two lots he has selected for his Tavern House. Hammond dislikes him and is anxious to know if you are under any obligation to sell him a share in the company property. I told him that I thought you knew Mann too well to promise him a mare. . . " (Hammond was a Kalamazoo banker who was handling some of the company affairs. Huntington was apparently the third settler in Richmond. The shoemaker was the fourth. The employment of Truman Austin to do some of the work originally contracted for by Stratton would be recalled later on.)

One of the two keepers of a public house, either Stratton or Mann, figures in one of the most famous tales concerning Richmond. It was recorded by early Allegan County historian Henry Hudson Hutchins, who heard it from some who were there: "The banking laws in the time of the wild cat banks provided that each bank should have constantly on hand a required amount of specie reserve, and

I well remember hearing my parents, in conversation with other old settlers, tell how it was arranged among a chain of banks along the Kalamazoo that a reserve fund should be held at a bank up the river where the state examiner would call first in his round of inspection. As soon as the reserve was counted at the bank the specie was sent on to the next bank in the chain by special messenger. . . On one occasion an Indian was taking the sack from Allegan to Singapore in a canoe and when between the present site of New Richmond and Singapore the canoe was capsized and as a result said specie reserve went to the bottom of the Kalamazoo. The examiner was detained at the place where New Richmond now is and feasted and treated until men could go with the Indian and fish out the bag, so that when the examiner finally arrive at Singapore the bank there had the required amount of specie reserve."

Shortly after the incident Hutchins relates the banking laws were altered, and the wild cat banks put out of business. This was one more circumstance that tended to dry up the money available for land speculation and economic expansion. It was a pinch the Richmond Company felt very deeply.

But optimism still prevailed. On January 4, 1837, a formal agreement was drawn up appointing John Allen "an agent to superintend and manage the business of said Company in the completion of said mill and the creation of other machinery and to make sale from time to time of lots in said village. . . " His commission was to be 10 percent.

In April of 1837 the investors sweetened the pot by giving Allen "entire control and management" for six years, and promised him half of all of the profits over $100,000, but added cautiously, "no further improvements than those already under construction without the consent of the majority of the owners. No charge to the company for traveling expense," and specified that Allen was "to be personally present on said property or keep a subagent there who is competent to superintend the interests of the company."

Several efforts were made to provide an on-site agent who could sell lands, run the company store, and superintend the work. In April of 1837 Moseley hoped he had the answers. W. Elnathan Bassett from "Juliette" (possibly Joliet, Illinois) visited Moseley in Ann Arbor and said he was interested in obtaining a share of the Richmond venture and in being their agent on site. He even had an assistant in the person of Reverend M. McCoy of Michigan City who was anxious to move to the property. Moseley contacted the other investors attempting to get up a bonus for Bassett. "He would be pleased in purchasing your remaining stock of goods on a credit provided he may have the privilege of supplying the workmen with such as they may want. Mr. Bassett says there will be wanted immediately whether you sell to him or not sugar, tea, coffee, chocolate, molasses, ready made clothing, course boots, shoes, one barrel lamp oil and lamps, tobacco possibly a quantity of

127

smoking [tobacco], But no ardent spirits nor even wine. Mr. Bassett wishes if you can provide two feather beds and a number of mattresses. The heathen Mann has already begun to keep whiskey and uses it freely himself." (The plan fell through. McCoy died as he was packing for the move, and Bassett abandoned the idea.)

Their financial problems were becoming obvious. In March of 1837, A. G. Hammond of the Bank of Kalamazoo penned an angry letter: "Since your absence, I cashed two checks of yours on the Bank of Washtenaw. . . and no provision having been made for them they are returned -- I have only a word to say in relation to them. They ought to have been provided for. . . I am also surprised that Mr. Moseley's draft for 500 dollars for expenses at Richmond should have been protested. The money was used for the Co. Business and ought to have been paid . . .unless funds can be raised in some way that can be depended upon, I shall be unwilling to have any money transactions come through this Bank -- It will not only afford me pleasure, but it will be in my interest to do any and everything I can to assist the Co. in their money transactions but as I said before matters must be arranged in a manner to be depended upon or I cannot commitent with my duty to the Bank afford any facilities whatever. I have been down to Richmond since I wrote you and am very well satisfied and gratified with the appearance and prospects of the city and feel still more and more confident that with close attention and proper management, it will be a grand Business place and one that will afford profit to the owners. System is wanted to carry things forward in a proper manner."

In December of 1837 Henry Morgan wrote despairingly: " We learn from our correspondent in Michigan that a portion, if not all, of our company lands are advertised for sale for taxes. What shall be done? We are prepared to advance one half the necessary amount and emplore some one there to attend to the same. . . We have waited very patiently in hope you would straighten matters to your entire satisfaction and we begin to feel that there should be no unnecessary delay in the matter." The taxes were paid on the village site, although many of the other lands were lost.

Sweetser made a trip from Massachusetts to visit the settlement and in a letter dated December 15, 1837 wrote Allen who was still in New York: "The appearance of the place now it is cleared off is altogether beyond my expectation, the ground is handsome for a town -- there are in all about ten houses. The Race is grubbed a mile, and the timber for the large mill mostly framed, but for want of funds the contractors have abandoned the job. The dam for the small mill is made, and the frame up, except the roof. It is very important that means be furnished to complete that -- say 150 dollars -- and my opinion is that if that amount was sent to Stratton for the purpose he would see it finished, and if you realize how important it is that the mill start you will make extra effort to have it done. When I was there he was raising his large public house. . . I like him very much -- he is just the man for the place, and will do what he can to build it up. Mann has built a good frame house.

"Unless work can be finished, I do not see but the settlement must be broken up, which would be very unfortunate. . . If the improvement can go forward I see no reason why the place should not realize our most sanguine anticipations. But if anything is done to save what has already been done, it must be soon. It would cost us a great effort to make a new start. About the time I was there the engineers surveying for a canal across the state came down the Rabbit River and into our bayou, leaving the Rabbit River where we contemplate taking out the water."

The surveyors were at work on the Clinton-Kalamazoo Canal, a project that had been approved by the Michigan Legislature in March of 1837. The planned canal would provide a navigable waterway across Michigan, linking Fredericks, near Mt. Clemens on Lake St. Clair, with Naples, a proposed town near the mouth of the Kalamazoo, and thence to Lake Michigan. The legislature appropriated $205,000 in 1838 to begin work, and ground was broken with much fanfare near Mt. Clemens, July 20, 1838. The canal was completed to Rochester, about 16 miles, when work was stopped. Later the 16 miles was augmented by bringing it into the Painted River. A portion of the canal and towpath later became an historical feature of Bloomer State Park. On the western side of the state, all that came of the project was the proposed town of Naples which soon appeared on maps and continued to do so for at least 20 years. Had the canal been completed, the development of central lower Michigan might have been very different.

A post office was opened in 1837 at Richmond with Stratton as the first postmaster and a Mr. Fairchild as the mail carrier. The plan was that Fairchild would carry the mail from Allegan down the river on a raft to Saugatuck once a week stopping en route at Richmond. "As a matter of fact, he carried the mail as convenience suited," the 1880 Allegan County History reported, " and frequently neglected the business for a month at a time."

By the summer of 1838 things at Richmond were at a standstill. Moseley wrote John: "I have just received a letter from Mr. Stratton saying that if he cannot be relieved from embarrassment by the first of April he must remove from Richmond. . . "

Less than two weeks later Stratton penned his own letter to New York and intimated that he was about to revive an "old favorite plan of mine" to found a colony on the Pacific Coast. "A man whose time is less valuable would do equally well here if the company does not drive ahead business. I wish a settlement to enable me to close my Michigan affairs so as to be ready for that or any other expedition, or if you insist on my standing by, I want sufficient funds to drive ahead and get through as soon as possible."

Ralph Mann was doing his part to advance the settlement. In May of 1838 he applied to Allegan County for "the privilege of keeping a ferry across the Kalamazoo River in the village of Richmond where the road from Allegan crosses the river." The ferry was to be open from 5 a.m. to 9 p.m. in the summer, and at 6 a.m. the rest of the year. Passenger rates would be 12 1/2 cents, a horse and rider cost 25 cents, cattle or horses 10 cents each, sheep and swine 6 1/4 cents each. His franchise was approved for three years.

In an effort to improve his prospects, and doing no good financially in New York City anyway, John Allen returned to Michigan some time in the summer or early fall of 1838. It is unclear from existing records and papers whether his wife, Ann, and daughter Sarah Ann, ever returned to New York from their visit to Virginia in the summer of 1837. The memoirs of Ann's nephew J. Marshall McCue, seem to indicate that she stayed in Virginia for a considerable period of time. John's daughter, Elizabeth, in her letter to her brother after she got to New York City in January of 1838 does not mention them, strengthening the idea that they were still in Virginia. In an 1842 letter Ann talks about the money advanced to her by her Uncle McKim "to pay my traveling expenses to New York". It is possible that Ann and Sarah returned to New York City for a short

132

time, and traveled back to Michigan with
John and Elizabeth.

By October of 1838 they were all
back in Ann Arbor, and Ann wrote her son
in Virginia in 1839: "Mr. Allen was gone
west, he was absent about three months.
We have been boarding since last
October. I did not know what his
determinations would be untill he
returned, he is, I believe, engaged in
superintending building two sawmills out
in a village he calls Richmond on the
Kalamazoo River, a company he says he
has interest in. Since returning he has
moved Sarah Ann and I to a small house
of James C. Allen, his son -- We live on
a small scale. He is gone again west. He
could not tell how long he should be
gone. He talks sometimes of living in
Ann Arbor, at other times going out to
this new place which I spoke of. Before
he started west he said when he returned
he thought he should visit Texas this
winter. His mind is as unsettled as
ever. . . He has given up the brick
house. We live as we can, adopting the
strictest economy. . . I am poor and
cannot command a shilling. I have to do
without."

John was on the scene in Richmond on
April 6, 1839, for the first town
meeting of the newly organized township
of Manlius. He was one of eight citizens
voting in the election, and was chosen
the first Supervisor. He was also named
Overseer of Highways for District 1,
and on the first assessment of road tax
for the Township of Manlius for the year
1839, he lists himself as one of eight
"residents." On November 4 and 5 of that

133

John Allen listed himself as a resident in 1839 when he wrote out this tax roll.

year he was an inspector at the general election where the eight Manlius Township voters were evenly divided between the Whig and Democratic parties. (The Township of Manlius was organized by an act of the state legislature, March 6, 1838. John had asked that the new township be named Richmond, but there already was a Richmond in Michigan, so John R. Kellogg, a member of the legislature originally from Manlius, New York, named it after his home town.)

James A. Poage was also present at that first town meeting and was named town clerk. Poage is not a name common in Allegan County. However, it was a very common name on John Allen's ancestral tree. His Aunt Ann was married to George Poage, his brother William's wife was originally a Poage, and his sister Mary was the second wife of Maj. William Poage. James Poage purchased a city lot in Richmond, and was listed as a resident on the tax roll of 1839. He was gone from the area by the November election.

John, in his attempt to get the mills going, apparently ran into other needs and asked the investors for additional funds. In July he received a letter from Sweetser trying to set things straight. Sweetser said he had conferred with Boltwood and "we both feel a reluctance at incurring liabilities in the present uncertain state of affairs, but we feel disposed to make an effort to raise the funds agreeably to your propositions, and to pay the same from time to time as the improvements progress <u>provided</u> we can secure the completion of the run and large mill. You say if you can have $4,000, you can with the aid of 10 or 12 shares and a few village lots complete the run &c." Sweetser also repeated what was apparently part of John's proposal that he "go to Richmond to live and to take the superintendence of our affairs there for five years." For these services he was to be given certain lands. He concludes the letter, "I hope to hear that you are appointed postmaster at Richmond."

But John Allen was not appointed postmaster. After Stratton left the post was given to Ralph Mann. According to the county history, once during his term he was advised from Washington that he had failed to make his "returns." Mann had responded that he hadn't made any returns because he had not seen the mail-carrier for a month. Postal records show that the Richmond post office was closed October 19, 1839.

On September 3, 1839, Sweetser who had apparently been asked for more funds, replied emphatically: "I never intended or expected to advance any money for improvements there -- and as you well know that I have said from the beginning I could not do it. . . I do not pretend to judge of the expense or practicability of the enterprise -- I did however suppose that after having "broken ground" opened roads, built houses, with the facilities now in the village it could not take twenty-three thousand dollars to complete what was already commenced. And upon which considerable money had been expended and was contracted by Stratton and others for fifteen thousand dollars. And now if there is a doubt of completing it with the appropriation named, I think it had better be deferred for the present -- for it would be very unwise for me to promise what I may not be able to perform. . . "

Although John Allen had been elected supervisor of Manlius Township (and despite his contract with the Richmond Co.) he did not spend much time there and his family remained in Ann Arbor. When building plans at Richmond were suspended during the winter months and a great deal of the time in between, John could be found in Ann Arbor where he was attempting to revive his law practice to sustain himself and his family. "I am poor and needy," Ann wrote during this time. "I cannot get the cheapest calico dress without someone gives me the means to purchase it (if Mr. Allen makes anything) which I doubt is little, he never has a cent to spend on clothing me. He makes out to feed us, that seems hard work."

Money was in short supply all over. Boltwood wrote in the summer of 1840: "The difficulty of obtaining money during the last six months has been much greater than I ever knew before. Our city papers speak of brighter prospects; but no individual feels any relief.

"You ask what is best for us to do with Richmond. I know not what to say -- I have no doubt but something laid out there in improvements would greatly advance our interest. But in the present state of things it is out of my power to make a raise.

"I had thought. . . that I had a fair prospect of raising funds by selling a portion of my western property, but thus far have been disappointed. Everybody in the East is afraid of Western lands, but the credit of Michigan is rising. . . but how soon there will be a demand for land at a fair price I have not foresight enough to determine."

Also in March 16, 1840 Truman Austin filed suit in Allegan County Circuit

Court against the investors for $1739.69 which he claimed as wages for "clearing land, labor, boarding guests, etc." The eastern investors who were apparently less used to owing people money than John Allen wrote that they were "surprised and troubled," and hired Allegan attorney Flavius T. Littlejohn (who ran unsuccessfully for governor of Michigan in 1849) to defend them. After a series of continuances the suit was dismissed in November of 1841.

Things were still difficult on the home front in Ann Arbor. Ann Allen wrote to her son June 9, 1841: "It is especially hard times in Michigan with every one -- Mich. money has fell, one dollar on the Bank of Mich. Detroit, passes only for half dollar (eastern money can scarcely be obtained) and people have lost all confidence in each other as it regards buying and selling. Very little business done on credit, so business is at a stand in this place. . Sarah does not go to school this summer. She stays at home and helps me to work. She occasionally sews a little for a friend and then they give her something which helps her along. So this is the way we get along in this troublesome world and I see nothing to cause me to think times will allter for the better for me. Sarah of course is young and may hope, but all my hopes are realized in disappointment." She also relates that recent correspondence from her uncle brought her the news that she had lost most of her money in an eastern bank.

During 1841 things were quiet in Richmond, although the company did receive some income from Abel Barnum, who purchased some oak timber to make staves. The price he proposed was 50 cents per thousand feet for the timber.

In January of 1842, Boltwood inquired about progress on the Austin suit and added, "Also let me know the present condition of Richmond. Have the taxes been paid? And what are the prospects of Michigan generally? I should be glad to know, definitely, what portion of Richmond, and how many village lots have been sold, by contract and to whom."

Perhaps to get answers to these questions John wrote Ralph Mann and received a reply dated, March 23, 1842: "I will endeavor to answer your inquiries. Mr. Ball is in Allegan he or someone in his family have been sick most of the time since they left. . . why they quit this place I cannot say. I have made inquiries to see if I could get any one that would take your place here but have not succeeded yet. there is a number of families coming in on the south side of the river this spring some of them may want it. Your hogs have done well I butchered the Barrows the other day he weighed 260 lbs. for which I will account to you for. as for your taxes I had made my returns before I received any word from you I have nothing on hand that will pay them but think I shall have and will pay them if I get the means. I am now very busy in Building a Bridge across the River at this place for which I am to have $700. The county pay $550 of it. I am making arrangements to build a saw mill on the south side of the River this season and will purchase

139

the Irons, Bars and Saw of the little Mill if you will dispose of them at a fair price. The Mill has mostly fallen down I wish you would write and let me know whether I can have the Irons or not as I intend starting my mill by about the first of Oct next."

For John Allen the Richmond dream was over by 1842. Ann, in writing to her son, Thomas, who had recently been married, related that they were living in a "very pleasant little cottage" but that the lease would be up in November. "I cannot tell whether we shall board (or what) as Mr. Allen does not communicate what his intentions are. . . Mr. Allen I think will leave for St. Louis in Nov. he wants to get another new home. How pleased I should be, if he was of a contented disposition. I know he could make a living here if that was all the object."

Taxes on the land were paid for the year 1842, but with no hope for industry the settlement faded. When Elam A. Fenn, the first settler in Fennville (four miles to the south) arrived in 1851, he reported little evidence of Richmond except for a cleared spot along the bottom of the bluff and the dug out portion of the mill race. Mann founded a small and short-lived settlement called Manlius to the south along Mann's Creek. The nucleus of families that gathered near the bridge on the south side of the Kalamazoo, across the river from the original Richmond, called their town Richmond, and prospects for the area brightened as the first railroad through western Allegan county in 1871 crossed

140

the river at that point. When a post office was opened there October 3, 1872, it was called New Richmond, because there was already a post office named Richmond in Michigan. A small unincorporated settlement is still located at the site of New Richmond, although the post office closed in 1979.

Politics and Religion

When the Allen family returned to Ann Arbor in 1838, their financial resources were still running negative. They had nothing, and owed a great deal. One of the reasons that John was reluctant to go to Richmond to stay was the necessity of making some kind of money just to feed and house himself, Ann and Sarah Ann. He turned to the practice of law in Ann Arbor, and his collected papers reveal a fairly steady supply of cases, nearly all petty assault, theft, or debt collection cases, not the kind to net a good-sized fee.

In addition to his Michigan debts acquired before his departure for New York, he had thousands of acres on which he could not even keep up the taxes. To add to the financial unrest, John heard often from Mrs. Broom, who was left in charge of one of the buildings he had purchased in New York, and was having trouble collecting rents. However, receipts in his files indicate that he was paying off debts as quickly as he could attain the means.

During his absence from Ann Arbor the village had become the home of the

University of Michigan. In March of 1837 a bill passed the legislature to build the new campus at Ann Arbor and in June the Board of Regents convened at Ann Arbor to pick the location. There is some mystery about the selection of site. On June 6, 1837, the commission chosen to review the site (Lieutenant Governor Edward Munday, Isaac E. Crary and John F. Porter) presented a report recommending 40 acres "on the farm called the Nowland farm." A motion on accepting that report was tabled by the regents. In the afternoon a motion to consider the report was postponed "until a survey of the land mentioned can be made." On June 7 Dr. Samuel Denton, a member of the commission, submitted an amendment that the university be located on the Rumsey farm. That amendment was adopted by a vote of six to five.

Wilford B. Shaw in his history of the University of Michigan wrote about the decision: "The chronicle of their session is tantalizingly brief and summary. For some reason they chose the Rumsey farm on a hill on the outskirts of the city, back from the river. . . instead of what would seem to us today to be the more beautiful location offered by the Nowland farm bordering the hills to the north overlooking the river." The first university building was not completed until 1841.

Having more experience with banks, banking, and money than most people, John Allen sought to share his knowledge and prejudices in a series of "Lectures on Currency" held at the court house in Ann Arbor in the winter of 1839. On

January 17 the *Ann Arbor Argus*
reported in a column headlined "Mr.
Allen's lectures": "This gentleman's
second lecture on currency was attended
by many of our citizens who seemed to be
gratified with the ability with which
the subject was handled. It is evident
that he has examined the question and
made himself familiar with it in many of
its bearings. The views which he took of
the present system of Banking, and its
effects on society were sound and
conclusive. . . yet there were ideas
advanced which we think would be
impossible for him, or any other man, to
sustain."

It was after a lecture that featured
a discussion of "credit as a medium
through which banks derive great profits
and through which they are enabled to
make their exclusive monopoly an
instrument of oppression," that John
Allen penned a letter printed in the
January 31 issue of the Argus: "At the
usual hour of lighting the room at the
court house search was made for the key.
. . it was not found. It seems one of
the Deputy Sheriffs had locked it up,
and either taken the key with him, or
put it where it could not be procured.
Whether this was intentional or not, I
do not know. I will leave that for the
public to decide. . . I will deliver the
concluding lecture whenever the citizens
of Ann Arbor will provide me a
convenient place for that purpose the
key of which is not under Bank
influence."

The concluding lecture was delivered
the following week and the newspaper

144

reported that it was "not as fully
attended as we wished" but that the
ability of the lecturer was acknowledged
by repeated applause. " Mr. Allen is a
gentleman of undoubted talent and these
lectures will gain for him a high
reputation."

With his newfound popularity as a
speaker he was asked to read the
Declaration of Independence during the
Fourth of July celebration that summer
in Ann Arbor and to address the young
men's Lyceum in Ann Arbor.

After all of this oratory, it was
only natural that politics would follow.
He had been a delegate at the Whig
Convention in January of 1838, but by
1839 had changed his party allegiance.
In the election of 1839 there were eight
ballots cast at Richmond, and the votes
were evenly divided in nearly all of the
races, four for the Democratic candidates and four for the Whig candidates.
In 1840 after John had left the area
there were only seven votes cast at the
election, consistently three for the
Democrats and four for the Whigs. In
October of 1840 he received an invitation to attend a Democratic meeting at
Ypsilanti. In 1841 he ran for school
inspector and was defeated, but in
September of 1844 he received the
Democratic party's nomination for state
senator from the Second Senatorial
District, and was elected to that
office. He took the oath and his seat in
the Senate, then meeting in Detroit, on
January 6, 1845.

The Senate in which he served was

unusual in that all 22 of its members were representatives of the Democratic party, which had carried the state for James K. Polk in 1844. However the Democrats themselves, were divided into four disagreeing camps. The office-holding wing under the leadership of John Norvell, former U. S. Senator, was on the wane following the fall from power of their leader. The conservatives were led by Gen. Cass. The radicals were described as "thorough-going reformers professing the purest type of frontier philosophy", according to the Whigs they were "anti-everything". The last group to form were the Western Democrats who were largely a product of the internal improvements issue, they supported state and federal money for railroads and canals. John Allen tended to vote with the radicals, but no one faction had a constant number of adherents on all issues.

From the very beginning John Allen was an active senator. On January 21, just over two weeks after he was seated, he offered a resolution to ask the committee on the judiciary to enquire "whether legal action be necessary to enable a party, having a claim against an individual member of a firm, to collect the same from the joint property of the firm." In February he presented a petition from Henry Rumsey and 14 others asking for revival of the law against usury, followed closely by a petition to pass a law making it illegal to bet on the outcome of elections. The 1845 session adjourned March 19.

In the 1846 Senate he was appointed

146

to the committees on privileges and elections, on enrolled bills, and on incorporations. At that time any business, public utility, plank road company, railroad, bank, or village that desired incorporation had to petition the state legislature, where the request was reviewed by Sen. Allen's committee and reported to the full Senate with a recommendation. He later told his colleagues that he thought considering each new company in the state took up too much valuable time and recommended that the law be changed. The unwieldly procedure for incorporation was one of the major factors that brought about a call for a new constitutional convention in 1850. The 1846 legislative session did not adjourn until May 16.

The *Ann Arbor Argus* had changed both its name and poltical affiliation and was known as the *True Democrat*. It cared little for local gossip, and carried very little local news, but covered with evangelistic fervor both state and national politics. The daily sessions of the Michigan House and Senate were given the by-line "Reported for the True Democrat," and were presented in greater detail than the official Senate Journal. It is probable that the Senate account was written by John Allen himself, even before he purchased an interest in the paper. In the middle of proceedings the writer would interject, "Mr. Allen hoped. . ." or Mr. Allen thought. . ." At one point in 1846 the paper quoted Mr. Allen as telling his colleagues, "Senators are not sent here to sit and want until petitions are sent in -- they (the Senators) come direct from the

people with their desires and wants
fresh in their minds, obtained by
intercourse with them while at home, and

State Senator John Allen, about 1847.

it is expected that they will remember
the wishes of their constituents and
adopt such wholesome and judicious laws
as the people expect from them. But
legislators, when they reach the city,
sometimes forget the promises they made
at home, and the measures of reform that
were urged upon them..."

John Allen's reform fervor at this time was directed at the Michigan court system. In March of 1845 he became part owner of the *True Democrat* in partnership with Orrin Arnold. The August 27, 1846, edition of the paper carried an account of "Remarks made by Mr. Allen in the Senate last session. The "remarks" covered the entire front page and spilled onto page two. In them he called for a "thorough and radical reform of the judicial department of state." One of the chief problems of the judicial system, according to the article, is that it was "copied from and followed the English. A system framed for and calculated to aid wealth and power to lord it over the masses." He said the system was "adapted and suitable for a country like England," but not adapted to "our republican institutions and republican habits." His aim was "to remove these evils and open the door for the administration of justice that will mete it out to all classes of our citizens alike."

The bill, in somewhat modified form, passed both houses in 1846, but was pocket vetoed by Acting Governor William L. Greenly.

In the opening days of the 1847 Senate "Mr. Allen gave notice that he would, at some future date, ask leave to introduce a bill so to amend chapter 89 and 92 of the revised statutes of Michigan of 1846, as to confer jurisdiction on the county courts for the trial of all civil and criminal cases, and to limit the jurisdiction of the circuit court to appellate jurisdiction from county courts on questions of law, and original jurisdiction in chancery, and requiring all testimony in chancery to be taken orally in open courts."

Clark F. Norton, in "Judicial Reform in Michigan Between Two Constitutions, 1835-1850," wrote that "the state court system. . . was subject to constant pressure for alteration, both in structure and procedure. . . One movement for widespread revision, that almost achieved its goals in 1845, was led by Dr. Samuel Denton, a practicing physician, with the able assistance of John Allen. Both of these men, residents of Ann Arbor, were elected to the state senate in 1845 from the second senatorial district."

The two major factors that brought about the decision of Allen and Denton to introduce such a measure, according to Norton, were first, delays in the disposition of cases, and second, the high costs of the court system to both litigants and government. Allen had kind words for the justice of the peace courts and other local jurisdictions, but called for abolishing the circuit and chancery courts, replacing them with a county court. He and Denton were opposed in their efforts at reform by many of the state's lawyers, some serving in the legislature. A portion of their plan was included in the general revision in 1846. A bill in 1847 succeeded in abolishing the chancery court. Another successful effort of the two senators brought about substitution of popular election for gubernatorial appointment as a means of selecting justices for the state supreme court. Some of their other reform efforts were erased by the Constitution of 1850.

When Michigan became a state in 1837 a decision on a permanent location for the capitol was put aside for ten years. When 1847 approached the legislature reluctantly prepared to vote on the question. In February the Senate voted with Marshall receiving the largest number of votes followed by Caledonia, DeWitt, Detroit, and Ann Arbor. No mention was made in the first vote of the site that later became Lansing. There was apparently a good deal of unrecorded wrangling. The next mention of the question in the official Senate Journal states laconically: "After much reconsideration the Ingham County site passed." John Allen voted no, Samuel Denton was among the ayes.

A frenzy of construction followed at the new capital site, then located in the middle of unsettled wilderness. Roads had to be built to the place, and a temporary state house built in time for the legislative session of 1848. At one point 30 buildings were under construction similtaneously. Workers labored through the night by the light (and warmth) of huge bonfires to ready the hotels and government structures needed to accomodate the lawmakers. The two-story white wood framed capitol, capped with a belfry, was ready by the opening of the session January 1, 1848, but many of the inns were not. State officials later described the nights they spent in barroom chairs, and on cots erected in their offices. Some were lodged in private homes until public accomodations could be completed.

The new capital had been named "Michigan" when it was located by the legislators in 1847, and the name was not popular. The joke that they were moving the seat of government from "Detroit to Michigan" and other similar comments brought about a desire for a new title. The Detroit Free Press in 1847 complained: "Michigan. This is the most indefinite word, just now, in the language, we believe; at least the indefinition of its application occasions us the most inconvenience ...this is an intolerable nuisance; and we hope the legislature will take immediate steps to abate it." It was one of the hardest fought issues of 1848. The House early in the session voted for a change to Lansing, the name of the township in which the capital was located. (The township had been named after Lansing, New York, which honored Revolutionary War hero John Lansing.) The Senate refused to concur. Instead they approved Okeema, proposed by Rix Robinson, an old fur trader turned senator, who was particularly fluent in Indian languages. The house turned them down. The second bill from the House which proposed the change to Lansing prompted the suggestions of Huron, LaSalle, and Franklin. This time Franklin was the Senate choice. The House would not concur. Other possibilities advanced in those stormy sessions included Pewanagowink, Swedenborg, Houghton, Harrison, Brushridge, Kinderhook, El Dorado, Thorbush, Marcellus, Cass, Tyler, Lafayette and Washington. As the end of the session loomed the House and Senate committees agreed on Algoma, but the full House would not approve it. On the last day of the session the change to Lansing was apparently approved (although the Senate Journal is very ambiguous about when the vote was taken, and what name was decided on, listing the bill only as " a bill to change the name of the Village of Michigan").

In November of 1846 John Allen became sole owner of the *True Democrat* and seriously in debt to C. N. Ormsby, owner of the local paper mill. Apparently he was also finding it difficult to serve in the Senate and edit the paper for on April 13, 1847, he thanked his readers for being "patient with irregularities," and added, "Since our return from Detroit we have had several applications for the purchase of our interest in this establishment and negotiations have been going on for that purpose in such a manner as to leave it doubtful who will be proprietor the next hour. . . We hope soon that the matter will be settled, and that our subscribers will have no just cause for complaint, as to the promptness of the issue, or of the character of the matter." According to the masthead Sanford & Brothers became publishers May 4, 1847. In 1848 it was sold back to Orrin Arnold.

In the session of 1848 John Allen introduced a bill to create a fund from the sale of state salt spring lands to for the support of branches of the state university. As a member of the committee on libraries he asked the state library for a full catalog of books "with statement of the missing volumes." He visited the state prison reported his findings, and introduced a bill to establish a state asylum for the deaf and dumb and blind, and also an asylum for the insane. During his tenure as senator a charter was granted Ann Arbor raising it to the status of city.

John Allen decided against standing for reelection to the Senate in 1848. There is some evidence that he considered running for governor in 1847. The *New York Express* of May 30, 1845, said: "John Allen of Washtenaw County is likely to be the Locofo candidate for Governor of Michigan." George Corselius, Ann Arbor newspaper editor, and a friend of Allen's, responded in his paper: "This we think, will not be the case, he is far too honest a man; John Allen does not profess to be opposed to banks and then go for them, and this will not suit the locofos; they must have banks." (In the partisan vocabulary of the day a Locofo was a Democrat with extreme political viewpoints.)

He may have had other political ambitions. In July of 1847 John received a letter from T. M. Perry of Mount Clemens reporting that he had submitted the idea to a colleague and "I can now say to you in confidence that this county would undoubtedly give you a large majority should your name be presented for the chief magistracy. In relation to other counties I know but

154

little and would rely much upon your own good judgement. (Judge Bell would be a candidate if you don't.)" It is unclear whether Perry's letter refers to the governor's office or one of the judgeships recently placed on the ballot.

In addition to politics these years were also significant because it was at this time that John Allen became interested in religion. Although it was his building that housed the first religious services in Ann Arbor, when the Presbyterian Society was officially organized in 1826, his name was not listed as a charter member, even though both his parents and his wife joined at that time.

In 1844 the Rev. George Field, a follower of Emanuel Swedenborg's theological ideas as embodied in the Church of the New Jerusalem, had come to Ann Arbor for a series of lectures. He wrote later: "The Court House had previously been engaged by a Methodist Minister for three evenings of the week; so on those evenings I was allowed the use of the basement of the Methodist church, a very ineligible place. . . But as this gentleman could not obtain an audience on the evenings I was lecturing, he dismissed his own meeting and came to hear me. . . I soon after preached several times at Ann Arbor, and always to a large attentive audience."

Swedenborg, who lived from 1688 to 1747, has been described as a "scientific and philosophic inquirer." He regarded himself as a prophet and herald of the world's final religion, although the Church of the New Jerusalem was not organized until after his death. The liturgy of the General Convention of the Church of the New Jerusalem sets forth as its primary doctrines: "That there is one God, in who there is a Divine Trinity; and that He is the Lord Jesus Christ; That saving faith is to believe on Him; That evils are to be shunned, because they are of the devil and from the devil; That good actions are to be done, because they are of God and from God; That these are to be done by a man as from himself; but that it ought to be believed that they are done from the Lord with him and by him."

The movement had come into being in Philadelphia in 1817 and gradually

Lucius Lyon

spread westward. Field reported that in Michigan it "was called the state church on account of our having so many persons holding office who were receivers of New Church doctrines." John Allen was baptized in the faith on February 5, 1847 in Detroit, but he had earlier accepted the doctrine. In 1846, he moved into the home of Lucius Lyon, a fellow believer, and former U. S. Senator, who had been appointed Surveyor General for Michigan, Ohio and Indiana, and maintained an office in Detroit. He wrote Lyon in November: "I feel grateful to you for the trouble you have taken to fit up my room, which you have too kindly offered me for the winter. I fear that you are giving yourself more trouble than my small friendship will ever be able fully to repay. We will be so comfortable and happy in our little circle, that I fear that the time of separation will be one of pain..." He added a note on the side of the letter, "Will I bring my AndIrons & shovel & tongs? I can put them into my large trunk as well as not."

As Field observed, many of those who held public office in Michigan were members of the New Church. John related to Lyon that the two naturally mingled. "Love to the neighbors, with all its details, is the true source and foundation of all our great Democratic principles. Regarding the subject in this light, Politics becomes a part of my religion...the love of neighbor is the very essence of Democracy. No affectionate receiver of the Doctrines of the New Church can be any thing else than a true Democrat."

Lucius Lyon was a Vermonter who moved to the midwest in 1821 as both a surveyor and a civil engineer. He was elected a delegate to the territorial convention at Ann Arbor in 1833 and nominated as delegate to Congress, a post he won over A. E. Wing and William Woodbridge. He served as Michigan's first U. S. senator in 1835, and is still the youngest man ever to serve in that office from Michigan. Since he was a surveyor he understood better than most the boundary difficulties with Ohio. and is credited with being the one who finally succeeded in getting the public to accept the compromise that gave Ohio the "Toledo Strip", and Michigan the upper peninsula. He founded or helped to found several cities including Schoolcraft, Grand Rapids, Ada and Lyons. Lyon Township and South Lyon in Oakland County, and Lyons in Ionia County are all named for him. He was elected representative to Congress from Grand Rapids in 1843, and served one term being named Surveyor General by President James K. Polk in 1845. He was on the first board of regents of the University of Michigan in 1837. Commercial interests included lead mines in Galena, Illinois, the water supply plant at Detroit, promoter of the harbor at St. Joseph, salt mines near Grand Rapids, and promoter of a canal at Grand Rapids. He died in 1853.

In May of 1847 John received a letter from Abiel Silver of Marshall, originally from Edwardsburg in Cass County, one of the earliest of the Believers in Michigan. Silver addressed him as "My dear Brother in the Lord," and says that he had been in contact with Rev. Field and "I have made him acquainted with brother Fox's lecturing and my own and also of your intentions. He thinks we are all disorderly and ought not to do so. . . In my reply I told him . . . that we were not interfering with the sacraments and things considered by the church generally as peculiar to the office of the Ministry. But that we were going about to lecture and exhort the people to holiness of thought feelings and actions and to point them to the true light of the Word as emitted through the New Jerusalem. . . Brother Field, I think will quiet his opposition when he finds out our only object is to do good."

Field may have prevailed for a time. A letter dated January of 1848 from U. S. Senator Lucius Lyon of Grand Rapids, also a follower of the New Church doctrines, commented: "I was very glad to hear last fall that you have commenced lecturing. I knew your ability to engage the attention of an audience and I did not doubt but good would result from your efforts. It would seem, however, that you have now given up the intention of lecturing and think you can be more useful in another capacity. Doubtless you have good reasons for the change, that I know nothing of."

By 1849, however, the New Church society in Michigan had voted to displace Field as leader of the flock (although he continued to speak on occasions). They ordained another pastor

to administer the sacraments, and named
a number of speakers to cover the weekly
services. John Allen was to preach on
Saturday evenings.

John   Allen

Wedding Bells

By the time John Allen and family got back to Ann Arbor in the fall of 1838 they did not own a dwelling house in the city he had founded. Ann wrote that they boarded for several months before renting a cottage. John's mother, Elizabeth Allen, had gone to live with her youngest son, James Turner Allen, whose second wife had just died.

Turner had married Abby H. Maynard, the sister of William S. Maynard, later mayor of Ann Arbor, in 1826. They had three children, Sarah Maria, who was born in 1826 and died at the age of seven, John, who lived less than a day, and Cyrus Trimble, born in 1830. In 1832 Abby died and Elizabeth took over the care of her young grandson. Turner married for the second time early in the 1830s, Abby's sister Maria. She had three children, Jane Tate, born in 1833; Abigail Maria, born in 1835 and died at the age of five months; and Virginia Maynard, born in 1837. Maria died in 1839.

Turner took for his third wife a widow, Ruth M. (Cone) Croft. They had three children, James Cone born in 1847 who died at the age of 20 days; Mary

161

Elizabeth, born in 1849 who died at the age of 10 years, and James Judson, born in 1851. Turner and his family later moved to Chicago, where he died December 22, 1890, at the age of 87.

Elizabeth Tate Allen once remarked that she had wanted twelve children, and although she had given birth to only

James Turner Allen as an old man.

seven, she had raised five of her grandchildren (two of John's and three of Turner's) bringing the total to twelve.

The elder Mrs. Allen was well liked and respected in the Ann Arbor community. In 1852 when the early women's magazine, *Godey's*, did a series on "The Pioneer Mothers of Michigan," she was included. The articles were written by Mrs. E. F. Ellert, with the assistance of "a highly intelligent and accomplished lady -- Miss Mary H. Clark -- who is the principal of a flourishing school for young ladies in Ann Arbor."

In speaking of the elder Mrs. Allen, the author wrote: "Mrs. Allen is accustomed to express herself in a manner so forceful and decisive, and at the same time with so much dignity as to evince talent of no ordinary kind. Speaking of a grandchild who was extremely cold in her manner she said, 'I loved her much, that is, all she would let me get at to love.' At another time when a young mother showing her little daughter, apologized for the dirt on her hand, as she had been playing in a sand heap, the matron replied, 'It will do her no harm. There is always rain enough in God's heavens to wash them clean.'"

The article also quotes Mrs. Allen as commenting: "When my son Turner was married he said, 'You have always given the other children a good wedding; I want you to do as well by me; and so we invited everybody in the village and had as good a supper as could be got up."

163

Mrs. Allen died July 14, 1861, at the age of 85.

In the census of 1840 the family of John Allen includes two females between fifteen and 20 (Sarah Ann and Elizabeth), a male between 20 and 30 (James C.), a male and female between 40 and 50 (John and Ann), and a male between 50 and 60 (perhaps John's law partner who boarded for a time with the Allens).

Elizabeth M. C. Allen, John's daughter by his first marriage, was married some time before 1848 to William Wallace Wilson. They moved first to Ypsilanti, and later to Markesan, Wisconsin, where William died in 1897 and Elizabeth in 1905. They had five children: Frank Seymour Allen Wilson born in 1848; May, born in 1854; Lillie born in 1860; William Heman Wilson born in 1862; and John Allen Wilson born in 1865.

James C., John's son by his first marriage, was married January 9, 1848 to Martha T. Porter, originally from New York State. They moved to Tecumseh and had at least two children, Mary, born in 1849, and Adelbert, born in 1859. James apparently died young. When Adelbert died December 10, 1867, at the age of eight, he was identified in his obituary as "the son of Mrs. J. C. Allen."

Ann and Sarah Ann continued to live in Ann Arbor, but John was seldom with them. After he was elected to the legislature he would spend the session in Detroit. There is in his collected papers a reply to his request to the

National Hotel for accommodations with a sitting room. In 1846 he lived with fellow believers in Detroit. There are indications that there were problems in the home. Ann wrote to her son, Thomas McCue, several times complaining that little money was spent on her for clothing. Following her Uncle Barry's death in 1842, there was apparently something due her in the will, and there are several letters between Ann and Thomas, and to a cousin, asking that they not inform John Allen of the bequest. "I have no doubt," Ann wrote "Mr. Allen will take the benefit which I derive from me." And in another letter she pouts, "He never consults my interest or feelings by words or actions, that is the reason Sarah and I take it for granted he would not be willing for me to receive the benefit resulting if he could prevent it. His constant plea is, he cannot get money, or he has none; and what he gets in trade, goes to supply family provision."

She warns Thomas not to say anything to the family, especially the Poages who are "cunning people." Ann relates that James Poage had "courted" Sarah Ann, but that Sarah Ann felt she could not marry a cousin. Sarah Ann herself wrote Thomas in December of 1842: "We remain in the house we occupy until spring. We are our own domesticks. I have become a thoroughbred housekeeper. I play upon the pots and kittles as well as the Piano. . . Men are such flirts there is no believing them. I have had a number of offers but something lacking in all, I am hard to suit (they say)."

Ann Allen after her return to Virginia

In 1844 Ann wrote darkly: "My situation here is very precarious as it regards my domestic home. Mr. Allen changes not."

Exactly when Ann and Sarah Ann left Ann Arbor to return to Virginia is unclear. A granddaughter wrote later

"Mrs. Allen returned to Ft. Defiance, Virginia, to live with her son since Mr. Allen had gone on further west and no word was coming from him. She was left with no support so her son Thomas sent and brought his mother and Sarah to his home in Virginia."

In the memoirs of Turner, he states simply, "Ann and John had one child, a daughter, her name was Sarah Ann, her Father and Mother not living happy together, agreed to separate and she with her daughter left Ann Arbor and returned to Augusta County." In references to John Allen in the Field history of the New Church he is often referred to as John Allen of Tecumseh, and some of his letters to Lyon are datelined Tecumseh, which would lead to speculation that by 1846 he was spending at least some of his time with James C. and family.

Most historians agree that both Ann and Sarah Ann were in Virginia, when Sarah Ann, then a young lady of 24, wrote to her father on November 23, 1847:

> I have come to the conclusion to marry. The gentleman of my choice is intelligent, a physician by profession; a man of exceptional character with habits and tastes congenial to mine. His family stands high as it regards respectability. He is a nephew of old Dr. Waddle of Staunton. His age is somewhat of an objection; he is some ten or fifteen years older

than me and I fear a rather delicate constitution, and what you would call decidedly homely; with rather too much independence and decision of character to be popular. His practice is at present somewhat limited as there are many to compete with of the same profession. But I think by the strictest economy and industry we will be enabled to get along. His profession is his fortune. I hope you will assist me all you can; for I do not want him to run indebt any more than he can possibly help, to procure a house and furnish it in the plainest manner. I have not succeeded in selling any piano; but I hope I shall. I want to help pay for the house and lot with it. I do not intend to have any wedding, just enough to witness the ceremony. I shall be married in the dress I wore when I was a bridesmaid in Michigan. . . I wish you could send me some money now. Perhaps you could make some trade and get something toward housekeeping; a carpet or two, a set of china or anything that would be useful. . . I expect nothing more from Brother Thomas as he has given me my board thus far. How is Elizabeth? How many children has she? Father, anything you choose to send will be gratefully received.

I remain your affectionate daughter

S. A. Allen

P.S. Father, I suppose you have no objection to my marrying that gentleman, give me your advice on the subject. His name is Dr. J. A. Waddell of New Hope a small town about 4 miles from here. The place is about the size of Dexter.

Ann's son Thomas had married and settled in Fort Defiance, Virginia, just north of Staunton. Her elder son John was often a trial to her, suffering in his youth from an unrequited love, and much given to the wanderlust. Both predeceased her.

After Sarah's marriage, January 20, 1848, Ann lived with the Waddells in New Hope. In the 1850 census for Augusta County the household of "J. Addison Waddell, 43, physician," includes "Sarah A., 27, Lucy G., 1, and Ann I. Allen, 53." A granddaughter remembers her as "small and rather frail looking, a very interesting talker and a good reader." Ann took with her to a Virginia a large studio portrait of John Allen that remains in the family.

Ann Allen died November 25, 1875, at the age of 78. In her will she left her estate to her granddaughters Lucy G. and Isabella B. Waddell, and her son Thomas' son, Edward McKim McCue, with her personal effects going to her daughter

Ann Allen's tombstone in the churchyard of the Old Stone Church near Staunton.

Sarah Ann Waddell. She also asked that "my executors shall take from the estate a sum sufficient, but not to exceed sixty dollars, to purchase two neat plain tombstones and to have the same with suitable inscriptions, erected over the remains of my late son John McCue decd, and myself." She was buried in the graveyard of the Stone Church, north of Staunton. Nearby are the graves of her son-in-law, J. Addision Waddell, who died May 2, 1880 at 74, daughter Sarah, who died March 10, 1883, at 62, and their young son Willie A., born January 11, 1861, died July 17, 1867.

On to El Dorado

As his senatorial career began to wind down John Allen cast around for a new job. In February of 1848 he wrote Alpheus Felch, former governor of Michigan, who had resigned in 1847 to take a seat in the U. S. Senate, recommending that a land office be established in the Upper Peninsula of Michigan, "at Copper Harbor or some place near for all that region". When the new office had been organized he rushed a letter off to Lucius Lyon asking him to write Gen. Cass, recommending him, also "since you are acquainted with the President himself, a letter directly to him for an old acquaintance would do much good." John wrote that he feared the position of register or receiver in the new office at Sault de St. Marie might be filled, but as they were speaking of organizing three districts in the upper peninsula, two to be administered by Michigan, there might still be a chance. "Such a position seemed to me, " he wrote Lyon, "to be one in which I could be, by the mercy of the Lord, useful to the Church and to my country."

The same month he received a letter from Lyon, which assured him "I have this day written to the President as strong a letter as I could pen in favor of your appointment to such an office as you have been recommended for, or even a better one, and have enclosed it to General Cass with a like letter to him requesting him to aid your application if he sees any chance of doing so. . . I most heartily wish you success, in obtaining some office where you can perform civil uses, and at the same time Spiritual uses also, by spreading a knowledge of the truths of New Jerusalem. It is by means of the latter that the world is to be regenerated..."

But about that time word began reaching the Middle West of gold in California, in the earth and in the streams, just waiting for someone to come and pick it up. In 1849 a number of Ann Arbor residents left for the gold fields. The February 22, 1849, issue of the True Democrat carried a letter from George Corselius, who had been associated with John Allen in the newspaper in the 1830s and was a fellow New Church believer, advising the adventurers of Ann Arbor of the best route to San Francisco. He recommended travel through the Isthmus of Panama and added that the passage had recently been made much easier by the establishment of the steamer Orus on the Chagres River. (The Panama Canal was not completed until 1913; a railroad across the land went into service in 1855.) "A sail vessel will make the expense less," Corselius advised. He estimated the cost as: $30 by steamer to New Orleans, $40 by sailing ship New Orleans to Panama, $10 to cross the Isthmus, and $100 from Panama to San Francisco, a total of

$180. He also advised travelers to bring their own tent, so they would not have to pay for lodging in Panama while waiting for the steamer.

By December of 1849, John was fully caught up in the California dream. He replied to Lucius Lyon who was still working on the government post: "I have only to say in reference to the proposition, that I could do well in taking charge of the matter as proposed. Still, as I feel at present, I think I can do better, by going to California. The Lord willing I hope to start in three weeks from Monday next."

And on January 16, 1850, with exuberant pen strokes, he wrote Alpheus Felch in a letter datelined, "Steamboat, New Orleans, Mississippi River" : "I am now on my way to the great Eldorado of the far West. I need not state that I will be under very great obligations to you, for letters to any acquaintances you may have in that region, or for any documents pertaining to California.

"How long I may remain there, will depend upon circumstances. At present, I fix upon the term of two years, as the probable length of my stay there." Writing on the back of the letter indicates it was answered by Felch February 23, and a letter of introduction sent to S. H. Chase.

John's traveling companions were Abner A. Welles of Tecumseh, William Wilson brother-in-law of Welles, and George Van Nest. Welles was a resident of Detroit as early as 1822, when his

173

occupation was given as "hatter." He was later Register of Deeds in Ypsilanti. They left January 6, 1850, and went by wagon to Sandusky, Ohio; by train to Cincinnati, and by steamboat to New Orleans. There they boarded a boat and headed south to the Isthmus of Panama, took a steamboat down the Chagras River and made their way to the Pacific shore, then north to San Francisco, California. From there they traveled inland to the area of their hoped-for claim, arriving on the tenth of May.

Before he left John had written Lucius Lyon : "You may expect to hear from me, should I be permitted to arrive there in safety, as I shall write to my friends, a more full and detailed account of all matters interesting to those, than I have yet seen from anyone." He was true to his word and penned at least three long and descriptive letters from California, that were reprinted in the local news media.

The first letter was published in the June 19, 1850, issue of the *Michigan Argus* with the editor's note: "The following letter from Hon. John Allen, one of the oldest inhabitants of the village -- contains much information which will be of service to those who intend going to the 'diggins,' besides gratifying to his friends to hear of his safe arrival."

The second letter was written to his mother back in Ann Arbor, and later published in the newspaper. It was begun on July 27, 1850, with additional notes added August 2. John gives his location

Steam boat New Orleans
Mississippi river.
Jan. 16th 1850

Hon Alpheus Felch

Dear Sir

I am now on my way to the great Eldorado of the far West. I need not state, that I will be under very great obligations to you, for letters to any acquaintences you may have in that region, or for any documents appertaining to California.

How long I may remain there, will depend upon circumstances. At present, I fix upon the term of two years, as the probable length of my stay there.

If any thing should transpire there, which I think will be of interest to you, I will most happy in its communication.

Yours truly
Jno. Allen

N. B. Direct, to me at San Francisco.

Letter from John Allen to Alpheus Felch
while John was en route to California.

as "Matsell's Creek, 4 miles from its junction with the Mercedes river at the Horse Shoe Bend, Maraposa County, State of California." According to California historians this is apparently Maxwell Creek near the Merced River in Mariposa County, where there is a Horseshoe Bend, not far from the town of Coulterville. The nearest major settlement was Stockton. The highlights of John's letter:

On our arrival we pitched our tent among the numerous tents we found there for it was, and is, quite a village of tents, and contains several hundred persons -- here there are miners, tavern keepers, stores, victualing tents, gambling tents, etc.

This village, for so it is called although there is not a single house in it, and hundreds have no other habitation than the shelter offered by an oak tree, is situated on a small but beautiful river plain on the bank of the river, some 40 feet above high water mark, and bounded by high and rugged mountains, covered with a shrub resembling the Cedar. The next day after our arrival we set out on a prospecting tour. That is, we purchased a pick, shovel, and tin pan, and commenced our search for gold along the banks of the river and creeks. In this search,

which is called "prospecting,"
when we discovered a place
that gold may have been de-
posited by the current in the
present or past centuries, we
got to work with pick axe and
shovel amid the rocks of all
sizes, from tons weight to
pebbles, and mixed with clay
or sand as the case may be,
and dug a "Hole" in the
ground, of greater or less
depths and extent, according
to the circumstances, and
"green 'uns," as we were,
generally dug inefficiently,
and with ill success. When we
arrived at the point in the
hole at which we expected to
find the gold, we there
commence the difficult and
laborious task of "Panning it
out," -- That is, separating
the stones and dirt from the
gold. Gold being heavier than
the sand and gravel, will
remain at the bottom and may
be washed with certain
indescribable motions of the
pan, and the dexterous use of
water. The stones are washed
and thrown out with the hands.
If no gold, or not sufficient
quantities, is found in the
bottom of the pan, to justify
working the hole thus tried,
or as said, "prospected," it
is abandoned, and another
place tried, and then another,
and another, until the hidden
treasure is discovered in
sufficient quantities to pay

for working. Inexperienced miners frequently spend days and even weeks prospecting before they can find a place to commence work, such was the case with us.

We went up and down the river, and dug hole after hole, and washed pan after pan of dirt without success. We labored on, and each day if it did not bring us gold, brought us a little nearer to it by knowledge gained by experiments. At length we thought we had found a place that would do to work. . . The labor of digging as well as of attending the rocker, is of the very hardest kind. No labor of a farm will at all compare with it. At this kind of labor we commenced, and after washing hard all day the first day, we found upon panning out, we had not obtained two dollars a piece. After trying that hole for a few days in hopes that it would improve, we were compelled to go again on another prospecting tour to look out for another and better place, or, in the language of miners, "one that would pay."

Thus we alternately worked and prospected for about two weeks, occupying our tent at night, and cooking ourselves. In one of our prospecting tours we came up the creek on which we now are, and found that we could do better here than we could on the river. So we shouldered our blankets, tools, cooking utensils, and provisions, and set out for this place, packing each of us a heavy pack over the mountain, one of the steepest and most difficult roads, or trails, in all this region; leaving our tent and all unnecessary things behind. . .

Our camp here for some weeks was an oak tree, our bed a blanket, and our diet, short cake and pork, washed down with water from the creek. Here we continued to work and prospect as we had done upon the river, but with rather better success, as our know-ledge and experience increased but never exceeding five or six dollars a day each. Some days we would be encouraged, and then the next, do nothing but hard work and no pay. And our experience is the experi-ence of all other miners as well. . . Occasionally a man or two will strike a richer spot than others, and take out hundreds of dollars in a few days. But such strikes are becoming of very rare occur-rence. . .

We have purchased another place. . . This spot we hope

179

will remunerate us better and will last us for some time. It is an extensive bar from which several thousand dollars have been taken, and which still prospects rich in many places. In a few days we hope to have this paid for, and to be able to commence making our pile, be the same great or small, as the Lord may see for our good. We have now moved our tent up and spread pine boughs and bushes around us to keep us from the heat of the sun, which begins to be like the weather of harvest in Michigan -- thermometer one hundred above zero in the shade. Mr. W. and myself are at work together still, and keep house, or tent, and when we do a good day's work we obtain an ounce or sixteen dollars between us. This is doing well and satisfied us. . .

A miner's life is the life of a wanderer. He can have no assurance that the hole that pays him well for his labor today, will pay him for it tomorrow. He dare not, therefore, do any thing by way of permanent improvement, to add to his comfort in his camp, or encumber himself with things that would cost more to carry about with him from place to place than their use is worth. For this season of the year, a man wants in wearing apparel,

nothing but one pair of pants,
two flannel shirts, a pair of
heavy shoes, and a straw hat.
For bedding -- one large
blanket, thick and heavy and
colored. Gray is best. For
cooking utensils, one small
frying pan for two persons,
one tin cup, one tin plate, a
spoon and fork, with a jack or
sheath knife each. . . When we
first came to the mines, we
had such ideas of permanence
that we purchased seeds and
planted a garden, and attended
it. But this was so late that
the dry season -- for there
had not been a drop of rain or
dew since we came, nor will
there be any until November
next -- overtook us. Our
garden is withering up, and
will probably perish before
anything comes to perfection,
although our corn is in
tassel, and our potatoes in
blossom, and our beans quite
large. We have had radishes
twice, which were very fine
and tender. The land is rich
and would produce abundantly,
if it had occasional showers,
as in Michigan.

The place where we are we
think is perfectly healthy. We
are all in perfect health and
have been ever since we came
into the mines. The atmosphere
cannot be purer. We hang our
fresh meat to the limb of a
tree this warm weather, and it

181

dries up but does not taint or
spoil. We use the water from
the creek, which is not cool,
but is clean and pure. We have
comfortable beds, and sleep
sound, with Hector, our dog,
at our feet to look out for
the approach of grisly bears,
Indians or Mexicans. . .

Aug. 2nd -- Since writing
the above we have had better
success than we have had since
we came to the mines. Each day
for many days our labor has
been rewarded by an increased
amount; so that it amounted to
28 dollars, or 14 dollars
each, the day before it was
$12 and the day before that
$11 a day. This looks encour-
aging, if it continues, but it
may fail us in the same way. .
. We have now for the first
time fairly commenced our
pile, and if the Lord permits,
we hope to continue to enlarge
it, until we are prepared to
leave for home.

There are two things in
the life of a miner that are
distasteful to me -- mixing up
bread and washing clothes. Mr.
W. has kindly taken the former
to do and I bake it; and the
latter I still perform myself
though at great labor, and not
very well. . .

There are many incidents
in the miner's life that would

be interesting to those who are occupied in quiet and peaceable employments, if I could paint them for you in the language of poetry. But this I cannot do, nor will I attempt it. It is a state of constant excitement. For where disappointment crosses the path of a true miner, he does not lie down under it, but rallies his strength for a new enterprise.

In a letter to a friend dated August 10, 1850, shortly after the completion of the one to his mother he was a little less optimistic: "Our sucess thus far in mining has been far below our anticipation when we left home. We have been in the mines now over three months, and have not been able to lay up $300 between us. . . I do not, as some do, estimate mining in this state as the only thing that can give it permanent wealth and population. . . Thus as a more healthy state of trade and business takes the place of exaggerated prices for everything, and men become sobered and in their right minds they will turn their attention to the vast resources of this state for raising cattle and growing food. The mines are but the entering wedges to open to us a view of these resources."

On October 24, 1850, he wrote from San Francisco: "Our hole gave out much sooner than we had anticipated, and we being also worn out in a great degree with hard work, concluded to leave the mines and mining, and seek employment in some other channel of industry. We accordingly, with the small amount we had laid up, set out for this place on the 14th of last month, and arrived here on the 23rd." They had purchased about 20 acres of land five miles from the city with 16 plowed acres planted to vegetables "cabbages, potatoes, tomatoes, beans, lettuce, raddishes and kale". The letter continued, "Our enterprise thus far has been more successful than we had anticipated. Three of us made the purchase, and paid one thousand dollars down and agreed to pay $1500 more on or before the 1st day of Nov and have already paid $1300." He wrote of future plans to add "fowls and cows, so as to sell eggs and milk."

He closed the letter: "My health has not been very good for some days, having a somewhat severe attack of the dysentery now prevailing here. The cholera is also in the city."

The April 23, 1851, issue of the *Michigan Argus* included the item: "We have seen a letter received in this city from a gentleman now in California under the date of the 5th of March last which says: 'Hon. John Allen lies dangerously ill and is not expected to survive many days.'"

Although the news did not reach Ann Arbor until the last of April, John Allen died March 11, 1851, in Oakland County, near San Francisco. According to a record preserved by the N. Gray Mortuary in San Francisco, he died of "inflammation of the liver." His physician was Dr. W. Gab. D. Gordon (probably a business partner) paid the mortuary five dollars for digging his grave in the Yerba Buena Cemetery, a spot now occupied by the City Hall.

In 1836, in attempting to provide guidance for his son, just approaching manhood, John Allen had written:

> I am aware how little young persons of your age think of education. We are not fully conscious of its importance until we feel the want of it. We do not feel the want of it until we are called upon to take our place in the social and political and religious world. Then -- if we are observant and reflecting we will feel proud of the consciousness of our own worth in comparison with those around us, or humbled by a sense of our inferiority. To be the centre or brightest star in the circle of our acquaintance. To be looked up to as the head of the multitude -- the orator and principal advisor of a neigh-borhood, ought to be the aim of every young man.

SOURCES

(The major repositories for John Allen material are: the Burton Historical Collection, Detroit Public Library; the Michigan Historical Collection, Bentley Historical Library, University of Michigan, Ann Arbor; and the William L. Clements Library, University of Michigan; with additional material in the Regional History Collection and Archives, Western Michigan University, Kalamazoo, hereafter given abbreviated references.)

THE VISION

p. 3 "exceedingly hopeful..." Samuel W. Beakes, *Past and Present of Washtenaw County, Michigan*, p. 680.

p. 3 "man of dreams..." O.W. Stephenson, *Ann Arbor; the First Hundred Years*, p. 14.

VIRGINIA ROOTS

p. 7 "hunting ground..." Joseph A. Waddell, *Annals of Augusta County, Virginia, 1726- 1871* (1902), p.93.

p.7-8 "Allen Family," *Annals,* p.153.

p. 10 "Tate Family," J. Lewis Peyton, *History of Augusta County* (1883).

p.10-11 "because there was no one..." *Annals,* p. 303.

p. 11-12 Civil War story, Works Progress Administration, *Augusta County, Virginia, Historical Houses* (1937).

p. 12 "being disposed to aid..." Allen vs. Allen, 1824 Chancery Court Records, Augusta County, Virginia.

p. 12 Crawford Will, Lyman Chalkley, *Chronicles of the Scotch-Irish Settlement in Virginia, extracted from the original court records of Augusta Co., 1745-1800* (Baltimore) 1965.

p. 13 Federal Census for Virginia, 1820. Augusta County.

p. 13 Children of James, Annals, p. 153-4.

p. 13-14 "he had lived without..." William Henry Foote, *Sketches of Virginia, Historical and Biographical* (1850), p.420-421..

p. 14-15 "500 acres..." Augusta County Deed Records, Book 50, p. 439, and Allen vs. Allen, 1824, Chancery Court Records, Augusta County, Virginia.

p. 15 Family history of Ann, J. Marshall McCue Memoirs, recorded 1888, Allen Papers, Bentley.

p. 16 Will of Dr. William McCue, filed June 25, 1821, Augusta County Will Records, Book 38, Augusta County, Virginia.

p. 16 Will of John McCue, filed May 5, 1817, Augusta County Court Records.

p. 16-17 "I could pay..." Fragment of letter in Allen vs. Allen file, Augusta County Chancery Court Records.

p. 17 Land and debt back to James. Deed filed July 28, 1823, Augusta County Deed Records.

HEADING NORTH

p.18 "The impression..." J. Marshall McCue Memoirs, Allen Papers, Bentley.

p. 18-19 "Mr. J. Allen of Virginia..." M. T. Williams to John Allen, October 10, 1823, John Allen Manuscripts, Burton.

p. 19 "great obligation..." () Harris to John Allen, December 29, 1823, John Allen Manuscripts, Burton.

p. 20 Cupid, William A. Moseley to John Allen, April 29, 1824, John Allen Manuscripts, Burton.

p. 20 Asa Mills Family, *History of Kalamazoo County, Michigan* (1880), p.381-2.

p. 20 "I am fearful..." M. T. Williams to John Allen, October 10, 1823, John Allen Manuscripts, Burton.

p. 21 "Your favour..."W. Williams to John Allen, February 15, 1824, Burton.

p. 21-22 Rumsey family history, Russell E. Bidlack, *John Allen and the Founding of Ann Arbor* (1962), p.9.

p. 23 "when about half..." as recorded later in "Detroit Thirty Years Ago," by John Bryan in the *Washtenaw Whig,* March 22, 1854, reprinted from the *Detroit Advertiser,*

p. 25 "to explore the county..." *Detroit Gazette,* February, 1824.

p. 25 "They were on..." John Bryan, *Washtenaw Whig,* March 22, 1854.

p. 26 "Report of the Commissioners appointed to examine the County of Washtenaw and to establish the county seat," *Detroit Gazette,* March 26, 1824.

p. 27 Plat of Ann Arbor, filed May 25, 1824, copy in Burton.

p. 28 "I am glad..." A. Bryant to John Allen, March 5, 1824, John Allen Manuscripts, Burton.

p. 28-9 "The boat starts..." A. Bryant to John Allen, April 28, 1824, John Allen Manuscripts, Burton.

p. 29-30 "The said John..." Allen vs. Allen, Chancery Court Records, Augusta County, Virginia.

p. 30-31 "absconded..." Augusta County, Virginia, Tax Roll, 1824, and 1825, Augusta County Courthouse.

p. 31 "You are the..." John Allen to Jane Trimble, February 20, 1825, copy in Allen Papers, Bentley.

p. 32 "I remember..." J. Marshall McCue Memoirs, copy in Allen Papers, Bentley.

p. 33-40 "We traveled..." James Turner Allen Recollections, copy in Allen Papers, Bentley.

ANN ARBOR

p. 43 "Ann Scofield Hammond..." Alger Buell Crandell, *Ann's Amazing Arbor,* (1961) p.39

p. 43 Dykstra, Lillian, "The Founding and Naming of Ann Arbor," *Michigan History,* 1956.

p. 43 "much addicted..." Crandell, *Ann's Amazing Arbor,* p. 42.

p. 45 "commonly written..." John T. Blois, *Gazetteer of the State of Michigan, 1838,* errata.

p. 46 "We arrived in Ann Arbor..." recorded later in "Uncle John Says So", by John Geddes, *Ann Arbor Register,* June 2, 1886.

p. 46-7 "Ann appears..." John Allen to Jane Trimble, February 20, 1825, copy in the Allen Papers, Bentley.

p.47-8 John Floyd to Hon. Gabriel Richard, May 17, 1824, William Woodbridge Manuscripts, Burton.

p. 48 "to purchase all..." John Allen to William Woodbridge, March 7, 1827, William Woodbridge Manuscripts, Burton.

p. 48-9 Memorandum, 1835, Allen Papers, Bentley.

p. 49 "In the latter..." Deposition by Titus Bronson for Harford case, 1835, Allen Papers, Bentley.

p. 50 "me own..." Memoirs of Granddaughter Phoebe McCue Bell, Allen Papers, Bentley.

p. 51 "When we left..." James Turner Allen Recollections, Allen Papers, Bentley.

p. 52-3 "Complaint has been..." C. N. Gardner to John Allen, June 10, 1827, John Allen Manuscripts, Burton.

p. 52 Bill to Allen & Rumsey, April 1, 1824, from F. & T. Palmer, John Allen Papers, Burton.

p. 52 "raised a first..." James Turner Allen Recollections, Allen Papers, Bentley.

p. 53 "It is now..." John Allen to Jane Trimble, February 20, 1825, copy in the Allen Papers, Bentley.

p. 54 "In 1826 the..." Bethuel Farrand, "Early Settlement of Ann Arbor," *Michigan Pioneer and Historical Collections,* Vol. 6, p. 443.

p. 54 "It affords me..." Charles Lewis to John Allen, August 10, 1826, John Allen Manuscripts, Burton.

p. 54 "Oh, how great..."John Allen to Jane Trimble, February 20, 1825, copy in Allen Papers, Bentley.

p. 55 "I think your..." William Bell to John Allen, September 15, 1825, John Allen Manuscripts, Burton.

p. 55 "it became necessary..." C. C. Trowbridge to John Allen, August 17, 1826, John Allen Manuscripts, Burton.

p. 55 Tavern license, *History of Washtenaw County Michigan* (1881), p. 220.

p. 56 "After we got..."James Turner Allen Recollections, Allen Papers, Bentley.

p. 56 "The boat is..." *Detroit Gazette*, April 25, 1826.

p. 58 "He came running..." *Godey's*, April, 1852.

p. 58-9 "To sustain yourself..." John Allen to James C. Allen, June 12, 1836, John Allen Manuscripts, Burton.

p. 59 "physically a very grand..." Lorenzo Davis, *Ann Arbor Argus,* January 25, 1884.

p. 59 "attention to the..."J. W. Torrey to John Allen, December 11, 1829, John Allen Manuscripts, Burton.

p. 60 "We have written you..." Peck, Walter & Carley, New York, to John Allen, July 6, 1833, John Allen Manuscripts, Burton.

p. 60-1 "Sir: The acceptance..." W. C. Little to John Allen, November 17, 1834, John Allen Manuscripts, Burton.

p. 61 "I will make no..." John P. Sheldon to John Allen, August 19, 1828, John Allen Manuscripts, Burton.

p. 62 "That you have succeeded.." Erastus Ingersoll to John Allen, December 24, 1829, John Allen Manuscripts, Burton.

p. 62 "I see you have..." E.P. Hastings to John Allen, January 4, 1830, John Allen Manuscripts, Burton.

p. 62 "As to the appearance..." E. Reed to John Allen, March 6, 1830, John Allen Manuscripts, Burton.

p. 62 "We are decidedly..." January 20, 1830, *Western Emigrant.*

p. 63 "a few bottles..." J.Q.A. Sessions, "Ann Arbor -- A History of its Early Settlement," *Michigan Pioneer and Historical Collections,* Vol. 1, p. 333-338.

p. 63-4 N. Y. Farmers' Fire Insurance and Loan Co. policy, 1830, John Allen Manuscripts, Burton.

p. 64 Federal Census of Population, 1830, Washtenaw County, Michigan.

p. 64-5 "I have seated..." James C. Allen to John Allen March 20, 1833, John Allen Manuscripts, Burton.

p. 66 Water System Contract, May 6, 1833, John Allen Manuscripts, Burton.

p. 67 "Men, freemen..." *Ann Arbor Argus*, March 12, 1835.

p. 67-8 "We found Grandmother..."John Allen to James C. Allen, August 4, 1836, John Allen Manuscripts, Burton.

p. 68 Account of James A. McCue, Guardian of John and Thomas McCue, August 29, 1839, Augusta County Circuit Court, Virginia.

VAN BUREN COUNTY

p. 71 "Having laid..." *History of Berrien and Van Buren County* (1880), p.494.

p. 72 "Phrenological Character of John Allen," undated manuscript in John Allen Manuscripts, Burton.

p. 73 Eaton Branch family, Howe, Shirley Swift, *Vann Buren County Genealogies*, p.58.

p. 74-5 County Seats, "Recommendation to his excellency George B. Porter, May, 1833," Regional History Collection, and *History of Berrien and Van Buren County,* p. 360.

p. 75 "John Allen, Allen..." Samuel Denton to John Allen, January 11, 1836, John Allen Manuscripts, Burton.

p. 76 Kalamazoo County land records, December 13, 1835, Library of Michigan, Lansing.

p. 76 "Pa is now..." Thomas W. McCue to James C. Allen, September 6, 1836, John Allen Manuscripts, Burton.

p. 76 "further providing..." Lucius Abbott to John Allen, April 9, 1836, John Allen Manuscripts, Burton.

p. 77 "You say you..." Jesse Smith ot John Allen, December 28, 1836, John Allen Manuscripts, Burton.

p. 77 "I sold my..." E. P. Hastings to John Allen, April 24, 1837, John Allen Manuscripts, Burton.

p. 78 "The cashier..." J. R. Haynes to John Allen, April 21, 1837, John Allen Manuscripts, Burton.

p. 79-80 Middletown, *History of Berrien and Van Buren Counties,* p. 456

p. 80-1 Agreement dated June 19, 1837 between John Allen and Richard L. Lawrence and Joseph Hunt, John Allen Manuscripts, Burton.

p. 82 "I have heard..." S. Denton to John Allen, January 11, 1836, John Allen Manuscripts, Burton.

p. 82-3 "Dear Sir I..." C. Osterhout to John Allen, July 21, 1837, John Allen Manuscripts, Burton.

p. 83 "I have had..."C. Osterhout to John Allen, November 21, 1838, John Allen Manuscripts, Burton.

p. 84 Van Buren County Circuit Court Records, Regional History Collection, WMU.

p. 85 Locate seat of Justice, *History of Jackson County, Michigan* (1881), p.304-5.

p. 88 Jackson County Land Records, Burton.

p. 88 Deeds for Taylor and Abbot, Benjamin H. Packard to John Allen, February 28, 1837, John Allen Manuscripts, Burton.

p. 89-90 "Dear Wife Companion..." Taylor letter, *Spring Arbor Township 1830-1980* (1980) p.21-22.

p. 91 "I am now suffering..." B. H. Packard to John Allen, December 30, 1836, John Allen Manuscripts, Burton.

p. 91 "number of essential..." William Smith to John Allen, February 28, 1837, John Allen Manuscripts, Burton.

p. 92 "we are about..." William S. Maynard to John Allen, March 11, 1837, Burton.

p. 92 "rights for constructing..." Jackson County Land Records, Burton.

p. 93 "Village and post..." John T. Blois, *Gazetteer of the State of Michigan (1838)* p. 364.

p. 93 "There was a rush..." Franklin Everett, *Memorials of the Grand River Valley,* p. 33.

p. 94-5 "In relation to..." Henry Morgan to John Allen, January 7, 1836, John Allen Manuscripts, Burton.

p. 95 Contract between Louis Campau and John Allen and Henry Morgan, March 5, 1836, John Allen Manuscripts, Burton.

p. 96 "As to our Michigan..." Henry Morgan to John Allen, April 4, 1836, John Allen Manuscripts, Burton.

p. 97-9 Early land records, *History of Eaton and Ingham County,* and *Early Land Transfers Ingham County.*

p. 97 Deed to John P. Huntington, July 15, 1836, Jackson County Land Records.

p. 99 Japheth Fisher, *History of Ingham and Eaton Counties,* Michigan (1880), p. 419.

p. 100 Early Deeds of Calhoun County, Michigan, Library of Michigan, Lansing.

p. 100 Washtenaw County Land Records, Library of Michigan, Lansing.

p. 101 "on an eminence..." *History of Kalamazoo County, Michigan.*

INTERLUDE IN NEW YORK

p. 103 "sales of public lands..." Clark, Dan Elbert, *The Middle West in American History* (Thomas Y. Crowell Co.: New York) 1937. p.163.

p. 103 "Your pa..." footnote by Elizabeth Tate Allen to letter from Thomas W. McCue to James C. Allen, September 6, 1836, John Allen Manuscripts, Burton.

p. 104 "Sheriff's sale" *Ann Arbor Argus*, November 7, 1836.

p. 105 "Mr. Allen returned..." Ann I. Allen to Thomas W. McCue, November 19, 1836, Bentley

p. 105-6 "We have arrived..." Sarah Ann Allen to Thomas W. McCue, January 3, 1837, Bentley.

p. 107 Agreement between John Allen and Richard L. Lawrence and Joseph Hunt of Oswego, N.Y., June 19, 1837, John Allen Manuscripts, Burton.

p. 108 "Lots were held..." Franklin Everett, *Memorials of the Grand River Valley,* p.43-44.

p. 109 "peaceable possession" mortgage agreement, May 18, 1837, John Allen Manuscripts, Burton.

p. 109 "Father, I have..." James C. Allen to John Allen, February 24, 1837, John Allen Manuscripts, Burton.

p. 109 "my business here..." John Allen to James C. Allen, August 14, 1837, John Allen Manuscripts, Burton.

p. 111 "If when you come..." John Allen to James C. Allen, August 17, 1837, John Allen Manuscripts, Burton.

p. 112 "only for the..." John Allen to William Woodbridge, September 22, 1837, William Woodbridge Papers, Burton.

p. 112 Patent application, John Allen to Lucius Lyon, January 11, 1838, Lyon Papers, Clements.

p. 112-3 "My health is..." Elizabeth Allen to James C. Allen, January 16, 1837, John Allen Manuscripts, Burton.

p. 113 "James C. thinks..." James Turner Allen to John Allen, February 6, 1838, John Allen Manuscripts, Burton.

p. 114 "will attend to..." John Allen to William Woodbridge, July 16, 1838, William Woodbridge Papers, Burton.

RICHMOND

p. 115 "This place has..." Map of Richmond, Allegan County, Michigan, Burton.

p. 115 "at the time..." Contract dated May 20, 1836, John Allen Manuscripts, Burton.

p. 116 "I am glad..." Luke Sweetser to John Allen, July 26, 1836, Sweetser Papers, Burton.

p. 116 Bill for maps from C. B. Graham, August 15, 1836, John Allen Manuscripts, Burton.

p. 116-7 Map of Richmond, Allegan County, Michigan, Burton.

p. 117 "if you operate..." Lucius Boltwood to John Allen, July 26, 1836. Burton.

p. 117 "put it into operation..." Memorandum of Agreement, also agreement to cancel, both dated November 8, 1836, John Allen Manuscripts, Burton.

p. 117-8 "excavation of a..." Contract with J.F. Stratton, November 15, 1836, John Allen Manuscripts, Burton.

p. 118 "In 1836..." Allegan Journal, 1878.

p. 118 "twice during..." *History of Allegan and Berrien Counties,* p.264.

p. 119 "to build for..."Contract with George Mayo, March 31, 1836, John Allen Manuscripts, Burton.

p. 119 "February next" Contract dated December 5, 1836, John Allen Manuscripts, Burton.

p. 119 "Mr. Stratton has..." Charles Moseley to John Allen, December 31, 1836, John Allen Manuscripts, Burton.

p. 120-1 Map of Richmond, Allegan County, Michigan, Burton.

p. 122 "Mr. Ball has..." James C. Allen to John Allen, February 24, 1837, John Allen Manuscripts, Burton.

p. 122 "I hope you..." L. Boltwood to John Allen, January 17, 1837, John Allen Manuscripts, Burton.

p. 123 Allegan County Tax Records, Regional History Collection and Archives, Western Michigan University, Kalamazoo.

p. 124 "Suppose from 20..." O. Wilder to Knowles Taylor, April 10, 1837, No. 51, Letterbook, 1836-1838, Taylor Papers, Burton.

p. 124-5 "I have just..." Charles Moseley to John Allen, March 30, 1837, John Allen Manuscripts, Burton.

p. 126 "The banking laws..." Hutchins, Henry Hudson, *Recollections of the Pioneers of Western Allegan County,* p.9.

p. 126 "an agent to..." Memorandum, January 4, 1837, John Allen Manuscripts, Burton.

p. 127 "entire control..." Memorandum, April 27, 1837, John Allen Manuscripts, Burton.

p. 127-8 "He would be..." Charles Moseley to John Allen, April 29, 1837, John Allen Manuscripts, Burton.

p. 128-9 "Since your absence..." A. G. Hammond to John Allen, March 28, 1837, John Allen Manuscripts, Burton.

p. 129 "We learn from..." Henry Morgan to John Allen, December 11, 1837, John Allen Manuscripts, Burton.

p. 129-30 "The appearance..." Luke Sweetser to John Allen, December 15, 1837, Sweetser Papers, Burton.

p. 131 "As a matter..." *History of Allegan and Berrien Counties,* p. 265.

p. 131 "I have just..." Charles Mosely to John Allen, March 4, 1838, John Allen Manuscripts, Burton.

p. 131 "old favorite plan..." Jno. Stratton to John Allen, March 17, 1838, John Allen Manuscripts, Burton.

p. 132 Ferry franchise, Allegan County Circuit Court Records, 1838, Regional Historical Collection, WMU.

p. 132 "to pay my..." Ann I Allen to Thomas W. McCue, June 9, 1841, Allen Papers, Bentley.

p. 133 "Mr. Allen was..." Ann I. Allen to Thomas W. McCue, July 31, 1839, Allen Papers, Bentley.

p. 133 Manlius Township Records, Regional Historical Collection, WMU.

p. 135 "we both feel..." L. Sweetser to John Allen, July 29, 1839, Sweetser Papers, Burton.

p. 136 "I never intended..." L. Sweetser to John Allen, September 3, 1839, John Allen Manuscripts, Burton.

p. 137 "I am poor..." Ann I. Allen to Thomas W. McCue, June 9, 1841, Allen Papers, Bentley.

p. 137-8 "The difficulty..." Lucius Boltwood to John Allen, July 5, 1840, John Allen Manuscripts, Burton.

p. 138 Austin vs. Sweetser, et al, Allegan County Circuit Court Records, Regional Historical Collection.

p. 138 "It is especially..." Ann I Allen to Thomas W. McCue, June 9, 1841, Allen Papers, Bentley.

p. 139 Oak timber, Abel Barnum to John Allen, May 20, 1841, John Allen Papers, Burton.

p. 139 "Also let me know..." Lucius Boltwood to John Allen, January 28, 1842, John Allen Manuscripts, Burton.

p. 139 "I will endeavor..." Ralph R. Mann to John Allen, March 23, 1842, John Allen Manuscripts, Burton.

p. 140 "very pleasant..." Ann I. Allen to Thomas W. McCue, August 15, 1842, Allen Papers, Bentley.

p. 140 Taxes, Manlius Township Tax Records, Michigan Regional Collection.

POLITICS AND RELIGON

p. 143 "on the farm..." Proceedings of the Board of Regents of the University of Michigan, June 6, 1837, Bentley.

p. 143 "The chronicle..." Wilford S. Shaw, *The University of Michigan; an Encyclopedic Survey,* 1942, p. 32.

p. 144-5 "Lectures on Currency," *Ann Arbor Argus,* January 10, January 17, January 31, February 7, 1839.

p. 144-5 Manlius Township Report of Election, Regional History Collection.

p. 145 Democratic invitation, October 13, 1840, John Allen Manuscripts, Burton.

p. 146 "thorough-going..." Floyd Benjamin Streeter, *Political Parties in Michigan, 1837-1860,* p. 31.

p. 146 Senate Journal, 1845

p. 147 Senate Journal, 1846

p. 148-9 "Senators are not..." *True Democrat,* March 5, 1846.

p. 149 "Remarks made by..." August 27, 1846, *True Democrat.*

p. 150 "Mr. Allen gave..." Senate Journal, 1847.

p. 150-1 "the state court system..." Clark F. Norton, "Judicial Reform in Michigan Between Two Constitutions; 1835-1850" *Michigan Law Review,* 1952.

p. 151 Senate Journal, 1847

p. 152 "Michigan. This..." *Detroit Free Press,* January 8, 1847.

p. 153 Senate Journal, 1848.

p. 153 "patient with..." April 13, 1847, *True Democrat.*

p. 153 "I can now say..." T. M. Perry to John Allen, July 3, 1847, John Allen Manuscripts, Burton.

p. 154-5 "They were held..." Rev. George Field, *Incidents and Reminiscences of the Early History of the New Church* (R. Carswell: Toronto) 1879, p. 105.

p. 155 "scientific and philosophic..." Piepkorn, Arthur Carl, *Profiles in Belief* (Harper & Row: New York) 1978, p. 657-8.

p. 155-6 "called state church..." Field, p. 134.

p. 157 "I feel grateful..." John Allen to Lucius Lyon, November 27, 1846, Lyon Papers, Clements.

p. 157 "Love to the..." John Allen to Lucius Lyon, January 14, 1848, Lyon Papers, Clements.

p. 158 Life of Senator Lucius Lyon, by Hon. George W. Thayer, Michigan Collection, Grand Rapids Public Library.

p. 159 "My dear brother in..." Abiel Silver to John Allen, May 29, 1847, John Allen Manuscripts, Burton.

p. 160 "I was very glad..." Lucius Lyon to John Allen, January 24, 1848, John Allen Manuscripts, Burton.

WEDDING BELLS

p. 161 Family Record by James Turner Allen, Allen Papers, Bentley.

p. 163 *Godey's,* "The Pioneer Mothers of Michigan," April, 1852.

p. 163 "Mrs. Allen is..." *Godey's,* "The Pioneer Mothers of Michigan" May, 1852.

p. 164 Federal Census of Michigan, 1840, Washtenaw County.

p. 166 "My situation..." Ann I. Allen to Thomas W. McCue, February 12, 1847, Allen Papers, Bentley.

p. 167 "Mrs. Allen returned..." Memoirs of Phoebe McCue Bell, Allen Papers, Bentley.

p. 167 "Ann and John had..." Family Record by James Turner Allen, (Samuel Smith Manuscript). Allen Papers, Bentley.

p. 167-9 "I have come..." S. A. Allen to John Allen, November 23, 1847, John Allen Manuscripts, Burton.

p. 169 Federal Census of Virginia, 1850, Augusta County.

p. 169 "small and rather..." Memoirs of Phoebe McCue Bell, Allen Papers, Bentley.

p. 170 Will of Ann Isabella Allen, August 18, 1874, Circuit Court Records, Augusta County, Virginia.

ON TO EL DORADO

p. 171 "at Copper Harbor..." John Allen to Alpheus Felch, February 23, 1845, Alpheus Felch Papers, Bentley.

p. 172-3 "I have this day..." Lucius Lyon to John Allen, January 24, 1848, John Allen Manuscripts, Burton.

p. 172 Route to goldfields, George Corselius, February 22, 1849, *True Democrat*.

p. 173 "I have only..." John Allen to Lucius Lyon, December 8, 1849, Lyon Papers, Clements.

p. 173, 179 "Steamboat, New Orleans..." John Allen to Alpheus Felch, January 16, 1850, Alpheus Felch Papers, Bentley.

p. 174 "You may expect..." John Allen to Lucius Lyons, December 8, 1849, Lyon Papers, Clements.

p. 174 "The following letter..." *Michigan Argus*, June 19, 1850.

p. 176-83 "On our arrival..." *Michigan Argus*, October 9, 1850.

p. 183 "Our success thus..." *Michigan Argus*, January 8, 1851.

p. 183 "Our hole gave out..." Letter from John Allen dated October 24, 1850, *Michigan Argus*, January 8, 1851.

p. 184 "We have seen..." *Michigan Argus*, April 23, 1851.

p. 184 "I am aware..." John Allen to James C. Allen, August 4, 1836, John Allen Manuscripts, Burton.

BIBLIOGRAPHY

Bidlack, Russel E., *John Allen and the Founding of Ann Arbor*, (The University of Michigan: Ann Arbor) 1962.

Bidlack, Russel E., *John Allen's Letters from California* (Washtenaw Impressions) 1961.

Blois, John T., *Gazetteer of the State of Michigan* (Sydney L. Rood & Co: Detroit) 1838.

Brown, David J., editor, *Staunton, Virginia: A Pictorial History* (Historic Staunton Foundation: Staunton, Virginia) 1988.

Chalkley, Lyman, *Chronicles of the Scotch-Irish Settlement in Virginia, extracted from the Original Court Records of Augusta County, 1745-1800* (Baltimore) 1966.

Clark, Dan Elbert, *The Middle West in American History* (Thomas Y. Crowell Co.: New York) 1937.

Doll, Louis W., *A History of the Newspapers of Ann Arbor, 1829-1920.* (Wayne State University Press: Detroit) 1959.

Dunbar, Willis F., *Kalamazoo and How it Grew* (Western Michigan University) 1959.

Dunbar, Willis Frederick, *Michigan: A History of the Wolverine State* (William B. Eerdmans Publishing Company: Grand Rapids) 1965.

Durant, Samuel W., *History of Ingham and Eaton Counties*, (D.W. Ensign & Co.: Philadelphia) 1880.

Early Deeds of Calhoun County, 1952, Library of Michigan, Lansing.

Early Land Transfers Ingham County, 1947, Library of Michigan, Lansing.

Everett, Franklin, *Memorials of the Grand River Valley* (Chicago) 1878..

Field, Rev. George Field, *Memoirs, Incidents and Reminiscences of the Early History of the New Church* (R. Carswell: Toronto) 1879.

Foote, William Henry, *Sketches of Virginia, Historical and Biographical* (John Knox Press: Richmond, Virginia) 1850.

Gildart, Robert, *Albion College, 1835-1960; A History* (Albion College) 1961.

Gwinn, Florence McKinnon, *Pioneer History of Huron County, Michigan* (Huron County Pioneer and Historical Society) 1922.

History of Allegan and Barry Counties, (D. W. Ensign & Co.: Philadelphia) 1880.

History of Berrien and Van Buren Counties, Michigan, (D.W. Ensign & Co.: Philadelphia) 1880.

History of Jackson County, Michigan, (Interstate Publishing Co.: Chicago) 1881.

History of Ottawa County, Michigan, (H.R. Page & Co.: Chicago) 1882.

History of Kalamazoo County, Michigan, (Everts & Abbot: Philadelphia) 1880.

History of the City of Toledo and Lucas County Ohio (Munsell & Co.) 1888.

History of Washtenaw County, Michigan, (Chas. C. Chapman & Co.: Chicago) 1881.

Howe, Shirley Swift, *Van Buren County Genealogies*.

Kekic, Nick, *A Fine Place for a City; Titus Bronson and the Founding of Kalamazoo* (Oak Opening Press: Kalamazoo) 1984.

Lane, Kit, *Fennville Area* (Fennville Herald: Fennville) 1983.

Lane, Kit, *Singapore; the Buried City* (The Commercial Record: Saugatuck) 1975.

Lane, Kit, editor, *Western Allegan County History* (Curtis Media Corporation) 1988.

Lanman, James H., *History of Michigan; From Its Earliest Colonization to the Present Time* (Harper & Brothers: New York) 1841.

Lawrence Bicentennial Committee, *Times Gone by in Lawrence, Michigan*, 1976.

Lorenz, Charles J., *The Early History of Saugatuck and Singapore, Michigan 1830-1840* (Saugatuck, Michigan) 1983.

Manassah, Sallie M., et. al, *Lansing; Capital Campus, and Cars* (Contemporary Image Adv. Ltd.: East Lansing) 1986.

Marwil, Jonathan L., *A History of Ann Arbor* (The Ann Arbor Observer Company: Ann Arbor) 1987.

Peck, Paul R., *Landsmen of Washtenaw County* (Liberty Town Press:) 1986.

Peyton, J. Lewis, *History of Augusta County* (Samuel Yost & Son: Staunton, Virginia) 1883.

Piepkorn, Arthur Carl, *Profiles in Belief* (Harper & Row: New York) 1978.

Romig, Walter, *Michigan Place Names* (Walter Romig, Publisher: Grosse Pointe, Michigan).

Rowland, Captain O. W., *A History of Van Buren County, Michigan,* (Lewis Publishing Co.:Chicago) 1912.

Shaw, Wilfred B., editor, *The University of Michigan; An Encyclopedic Survey* (University of Michigan Press:Ann Arbor) 1942.

Sobol, Robert, *Panic on Wall Street; A History of America's Financial Disasters* (Macmillan Co.: New York) 1968.

Spring Arbor Historical Committee, *Spring Arbor Township 1830-1980; Reminiscing Thru a Hundred and Fifty Years* (Spring Arbor Historical Committee) 1980.

Stephenson, O. W., *Ann Arbor; The First Hundred Years*, (Ann Arbor Chamber of Commerce) 1927.

Streeter, Floyd Benjamin, *Political Parties in Michigan 1837-1860* (Michigan Historical Commission: Lansing) 1918.

Waddell, Joseph A., *Annals of Augusta County from 1726 to 1871* (C. J. Carrier Co.: Harrisburg, Virginia) 1901, 1972.

Wilson, Howard McKnight, *The Tinkling Springs: Headwater of Freedom* (Tinkling Springs and Hermitage Presbyterian Churches: Fishersville, Virginia) 1954.

Works Progress Administration of Virginia, *Augusta County, Virginia, Historic Houses,* 1937.

INDEX

PAVILION PRESS
P.O. Box 250
Douglas, Mi 49406

WESTERN ALLEGAN COUNTY HISTORY

Thousands of pictures, topical history of area, township by township survey of settlements, recollections, and more than 900 family histories.
537 pp, 9 x 12 hardbound with full color cover painting, indexed.
$64.50, plus $3.50 shipping

RECOLLECTIONS OF THE PIONEERS OF WESTERN ALLEGAN COUNTY
By Henry Hudson Hutchins

A resetting of newspaper articles written by Mr. Hutchins beginning in 1919, following interviews with "oldtimers." Softbound, 8 1/2 x 11, 54pp, indexed.
$3.00 plus 80 cents shipping.

PIERS, PANCAKES & PEOPLE
By Jeanne Hallgren

A history of Glenn, on the shores of Lake Michigan. Well illustrated. Softbound, 8 1/2 x 11, 63pp, indexed.
$9.00 plus 80 cents shipping.

* * *

FENNVILLE; THE EARLY YEARS

Profusely illustrated history of the Allegan County settlement of Fennville from its beginnings to about 1900. Softbound, 8 1/2 x 11, 52pp.

FENNVILLE; VILLAGE TO CITY

The story of Fennville from about 1900 to the present. Includes the 1933 bank robbery, and highlights of area fruit growing. Softbound, 8 1/2 x 11, 60 pp.

FENNVILLE AREA

Western Allegan county settlements near Fennville, past and present. Includes Richmond, Pier Cove, Glenn, Pearl, Pullman, and many others. Softbound, 64pp, 8 1/2 x 11.

Each book $3 plus 80 cents shipping.

By Kit Lane

Also available from Pavilion Press:

SOME STORIES OF HOLLAND HARBOR

The wreck of the Alpena, the Argo aground, the fire on the South American, and other stories. Many first-time published photographs. Softbound, 20pp, 8 1/2 x 11.
$2.00 plus shipping.

SINGAPORE; THE BURIED CITY

The story of the ghost town that existed on the shores of Lake Michigan, 1836 - 1875. Many illustrations. Softcover, 8 1/2 x 11, 24pp, indexed.
$2.00 plus shipping.

SAUGATUCK; A BRIEF HISTORY ILLUSTRATED

The history of Saugatuck from its early lumbering and fur trading days, through the era of shipbuilding, and its beginnings as a summer resort town. 8 1/2 x 11, 20 pp, softbound.
$2.00 plus shipping.

SHIPWRECKS OF THE SAUGATUCK AREA

Includes the loss of two ships named Milwaukee, diving for the treasure of the Pewabic, the storm of 1883, and the story of the Chicora and the tug Gotham. Softbound, 20 pages, many pictures.
$2.00 plus shipping.

THE BIG PAVILION

Pictures and tales of the big red dance pavilion at Saugatuck, center of west Michigan social life, 1909-1960. Softcover, 8 1/2 x 11, 20pp.
$2.00 plus shipping.

DOUGLAS; VILLAGE OF FRIENDLINESS

Founded in 1847 across the Kalamazoo River from Saugatuck, Douglas was a center of early lumbering and fruit growing. Softbound, 28pp, 8 1/2 x 11.
$2.00 plus shipping.

BY KIT LANE